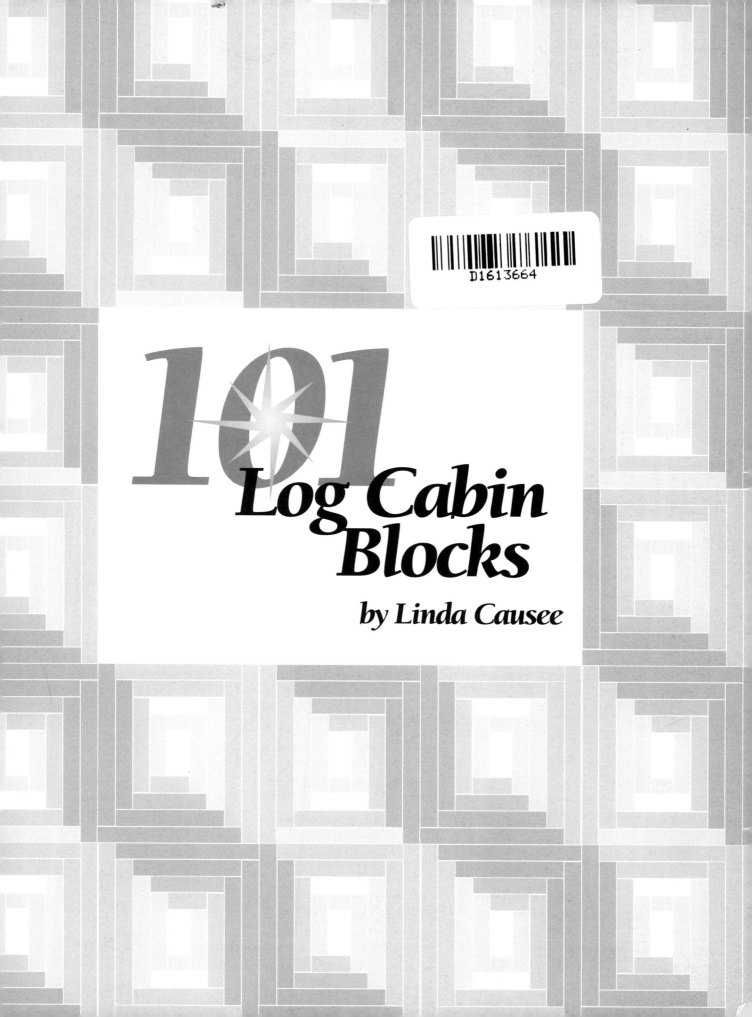

101

Log Cabin Blocks

by Linda Causee

Bobbie Matela, Managing Editor

Carol Wilson Mansfield, Art Director

Meredith Montross, Associate Editor

Christina Wilson, Assistant Editor

Terea Mitchell, Illustrations

Graphic Solutions inc-chgo, Book Design

For a full-color catalog
including books
on quilting, write to:

American School of Needlework®
Consumer Division
1455 Linda Vista Drive
San Marcos, CA 92069

Fabric was generously supplied by
Classic Traditions and Rose & Hubble.

Photographed blocks were sewn by
Linda Causee, Ann Harnden,
Candy Matthews, Meredith Montross, Pam
Nichols, Kerry Smith, Kathy Wesley and
Christina Wilson.

Introduction

Everyone who loves Log Cabin blocks will love owning this book! Not only does it include the traditional Log Cabin block (in four sizes), it takes the Log Cabin out of the past and into a new creative realm of innovative block design.

Linda Causee has twisted the logs and changed the usual rectangular strip shape—making this the most exciting collection of Log Cabin blocks ever! She's included new blocks where the logs become flowers, houses, hearts and even animals. She has definitely stretched the definition of a Log Cabin block being strips (or logs) added around a center square.

Using our foundation method for piecing, you don't have to worry about exact cutting of any weird shapes or tedious matching of points. Pieces are added to a foundation using a stitch-and-flip-open technique where all you have to do is stitch on the line. We have also included instructions for planning and finishing quilts using Log Cabin blocks so that you will be able to successfully complete your own unique quilt.

101 Log Cabin Blocks

A Little History

When one thinks about the history of the Log Cabin quilt, one usually thinks about the pioneers of the nineteenth century who lived in log cabin houses. The Log Cabin block was a symbol of their home. The strips were sewn around a center just as logs were built around a central hearth. The centers of the Log Cabin blocks were often red which symbolized the chimney as a source of warmth. Yellow was also commonly used in the center squares to represent the lantern as a welcoming gesture. The blocks were most often done with dark fabrics on two adjacent sides and light fabrics on the other two sides. They arranged the blocks in wonderful settings—some of which had their own names—Barn Raising, Straight Furrows, and Sunshine and Shadows. See illustrations on page 6 and 7.

The women made these utilitarian quilts from whatever material they had available—worn clothing, flour sacks, worn bedding and leftover scraps from their sewing. By making Log Cabin quilts, they made the best use of the fabric they had since they were able to use some fairly small pieces for the "logs."

About Our Blocks

The Log Cabin blocks in this collection range from the very traditional to the very modern. Five of the more traditional Log Cabin blocks come in four sizes, 4", 5", 6" and 7". There are also blocks that measure 6" x 8" and 7" x 8", but most of them are 7" square.

Foundation Piecing

The easiest and most accurate way to piece Log Cabin blocks is the foundation method. It eliminates the need to cut out each piece exactly.

Your first consideration is what type of foundation to use for piecing your blocks. There are several options. A light-colored, lightweight cotton fabric or muslin are popular choices. A lightweight fabric needs to be light enough to see through to trace onto and will give extra stability to your blocks. Of course, it will add another layer of fabric which you will have to quilt through. This extra thickness is a consideration only if you plan to do hand quilting. Another choice for foundations is paper. Use any paper that you can see through (notebook paper, copy paper, newsprint, or computer paper) for easy tracing, then tear it away after sewing is completed. A third choice is Tear Away® or Fun-dation™ translucent non-woven material. Like, muslin, it is light enough to see through for tracing, but like paper, it can later be easily removed before quilting.

Mirror Images

Log Cabin blocks, in general, are not symmetrical, therefore a mirror image of the block pattern will be produced when pieced, **Fig 1**. On each pattern page (pages 12 to 116), there is a small diagram showing how the block will look once it has been pieced.

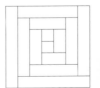

Fig 1

Note whether it is a mirror image of the block pattern and take that into consideration when choosing fabric and planning your quilt layout.

Preparing the Foundation

Tracing the Block

Trace the block pattern carefully onto your chosen foundation material. Use a ruler and a fine-point permanent marker to make straight lines and be sure to include all numbers. Draw a line ¼" from the outside edges of the block, **Fig 2**; cut along this outside drawn line. Repeat for the needed number of blocks for your quilt.

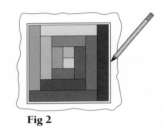

Fig 2

Hint: *If you want your finished block to have the same direction as the block pattern (for example, if you want the finished Log Cabin block #2 to spin in a counterclockwise direction rather than a clockwise direction), you must first trace onto tracing paper, then flop pattern and trace onto foundation material,* **Fig 3**.

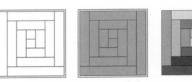

Fig 3   **Flop and trace onto foundation**

Transferring the Block

The block pattern can also be transferred onto foundation material using a transfer pen or pencil. Trace the block pattern onto paper using a transfer pen or pencil. Then, following manufacturer's directions, iron transfer onto foundation material. Write numbers on foundation using a fine-point permanent marking pen. The block, when pieced, will look like the pattern as it appears in the book, but will be a mirror image to the completed block shown in the color photographs.

Hint: If you want your Log Cabin block to look like the completed block shown in color and you are using a transfer pen or pencil (for example, you want the Log Cabin block #2 to spin clockwise), transfer as described above. But, if you would like your Log Cabin block #2 to spin counterclockwise, you must trace first with a permanent pen onto tracing paper, flop the traced design and trace again with the transfer pen or pencil.

Fabric

We recommend using 100% cotton fabric for piecing the Log Cabin blocks. By using cotton rather than cotton/polyester blends, the pieces will respond better to finger pressing.

Pre-washing fabric is not necessary, but it is necessary to test your fabric to make certain that the fabric is colorfast and preshrunk (don't trust those manufacturer's labels). Start by cutting a 2"-wide strip (cut crosswise) of each of the fabrics that you have selected for your quilt. To determine whether the fabric is colorfast, put each strip separately into a clean bowl of extremely hot water, or hold the fabric strip under hot running water. If your fabric bleeds a great deal, all is not necessarily lost. It might only be necessary to wash all of that fabric until all of the excess dye has washed out. Fabrics which continue to bleed after they have been washed several times should be eliminated.

To test for shrinkage, take each saturated strip and iron it dry with a hot iron. When the strip is completely dry, measure and compare it to your original 2" measurements. If all of your fabric

strips shrink about the same amount, then you really have no problem. When you wash your finished quilt, you may achieve the puckered look of an antique quilt. If you do not want this look, you will have to wash and dry all of the fabric before beginning so that shrinkage is no longer a problem. If only one of your fabrics is shrinking more than the others, it will have to be washed and dried, or discarded.

Cutting the Fabric

The beauty of foundation piecing is that you do not have to cut every exact piece for every block. You can use strips, rectangles, squares or any odd-shaped scrap for piecing. You do have to be careful to use a piece of fabric that is at least 1/4" larger on all sides than the space it is to cover. Triangle shapes can be a little tricky to piece. Use generous-sized fabric pieces and be careful when positioning the pieces onto the foundation. You do waste some fabric this way, but the time it saves in cutting will be worth it in the end.

Hint: Cut strips the width needed for the spaces on the block. Stack strips in numerical order to make piecing easier and quicker.

Foundation Piecing

1. Prepare foundations as described in Preparing the Foundation, page 4.

2. Turn foundation with unmarked side facing you and position piece 1 over the space marked 1 on the foundation. Hold foundation up to a light source to make sure that fabric overlaps at least 1/4" on all sides of space 1, **Fig 4**; pin or glue in place with a glue stick. **Note:** *Use only a small dab of glue to hold fabric in place.*

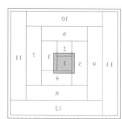
Fig 4

3. Place fabric piece 2 right sides together with piece 1. **Note:** *Double check to see if fabric piece chosen will cover space 2 completely by folding over along line between space 1 and 2, **Fig 5**.*

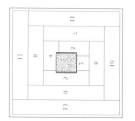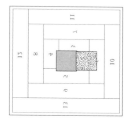
Fig 5

4. Turn foundation with marked side facing you and fold foundation forward along line between spaces 1 and 2; trim both pieces about 1/4" above fold line, **Fig 6**.

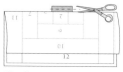
Fig 6

5. With marked side of foundation still facing you and using a very small stitch (to allow for easier paper removal), sew along line between spaces 1 and 2, **Fig 7**; begin and end two to three stitches beyond line.

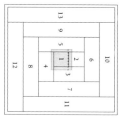
Fig 7

6. Turn foundation over. Open piece 2 and finger press seam, **Fig 8**. Use a pin or a dab of glue stick to hold piece in place.

Fig 8

7. Turn foundation with marked side facing you; fold foundation forward along line between spaces 2 and 3 and trim piece 2 about ¼" from fold, **Fig 9**.

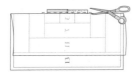

Fig 9

8. Place fabric 3 right side down even with just-trimmed edge, **Fig 10**.

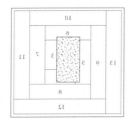

Fig 10

9. Turn foundation to marked side and sew along line between spaces 2 and 3; begin and end sewing 2 or 3 stitches beyond line, **Fig 11**.

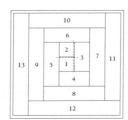

Fig 11

10. Turn foundation over, open piece 3 and finger press seam, **Fig 12**. Glue or pin in place.

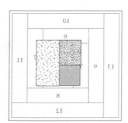

Fig 12

11. Turn foundation with marked side facing you; fold foundation forward along line between spaces 1, 3 and 4. If previous stitching makes it difficult to fold foundation forward, pull paper foundation away from fabric at stitching, then fold along line. If using a fabric foundation, fold it forward as far as it will go and trim to about ¼" from drawn line, **Fig 13**.

Fig 13

12. Sew along line between spaces 1, 3 and 4, **Fig 14**.

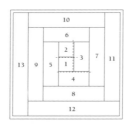

Fig 14

13. Continue trimming and sewing pieces in numerical order until block is complete, **Fig 15**. Press block, then trim fabric even with outside line of foundation to complete block, **Fig 16**.

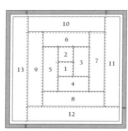

Fig 15

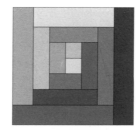

Fig 16

Planning a Quilt

The variety of sizes of the Log Cabin blocks in this book allows for a wide range of quilts sizes. You can make small wall hangings as well as bed quilts.

Wall Hangings

To make a wall hanging, you can place sixteen blocks together and get the following sizes (without borders):

4" blocks for a 16" x 16" quilt

5" blocks for a 20" x 20" quilt

6" blocks for a 24" x 24" quilt

7" blocks for a 28" x 28" quilt

6" x 8" blocks for a 24" x 32" quilt

The blocks can be placed in a variety of settings, **Fig 17**.

Fig 17 - Barn Raising

Fig 17 - Sunshine and Shadows

Fig 17 - Straight Furrows

Fig 17 - Star

ed Quilts

etermine the size bed quilt you are making using the fol-
wing chart as a guide.

Bed Size	Mattress Size
Crib	27" x 51"
Twin	39" x 75"
Double	54" x 75"
Queen	60" x 80"
King	76" x 80"

o the mattress size, add the desired drop (the part of the
uilt that hangs over the edge of the mattress). If a tuck is
esired (the part that is tucked under the pillows), also add
at amount. For example, if you want your quilt to hang
2" over the edge of the mattress with a 12" tuck, add 24" to
e length and width of the mattress size.

nce you have figured out how big your quilt will have to
e, you will need to choose your block(s). If you use 7"
quare blocks, and want a traditional Log Cabin look, use 96

blocks (# 92) set 8 across and 12 down with a 2" and a 6"
border to make a quilt with a finished size of 72" x 100",
Fig 18.

Fig 18 - Quilt Layout 1

Or, you can make a quilt with the rectangular 7" x 8" block
(#37) and use only 80 blocks set 8 across and 10 down with
a 2" and a 6" border to make a quilt with a finished size of
72" x 96", **Fig 19**.

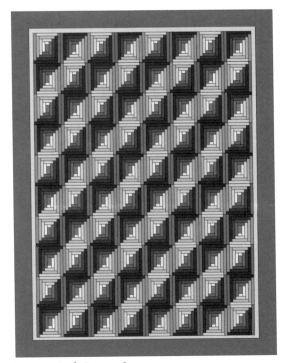

Fig 19 - Quilt Layout 2

7

Some of the square Log Cabin blocks can be set on point. If you use a 7" block, cut two 5½" squares in half diagonally and sew the triangles onto each side of the block, **Fig 20**. The block will now have a finished size of 9⅞".

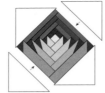

Fig 20 - Block #86

For a quilt with the new block size, you could use 48 blocks set 6 across and 8 down with a 3" and a 6" border to make a quilt with a finished size of 77¼" x 97", **Fig 21**.

With the same block, you could add 2" sashing strips an only use 35 blocks set 5 across and 7 down with 2" and 5 borders to make a quilt with a finished size of 71⅜" x 95⅛" **Fig 22**.

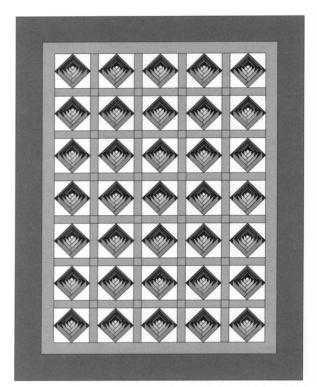

Fig 22 - Quilt Layout 4

Fig 21 - Quilt Layout 3

For quilts in other bed sizes, follow the quilt layouts in **Figs 18 to 22** and see chart below.

Layout	Twin	Full	Queen	King
Quilt Layout 1	60" x 102"	74" x 102"	80" x 108"	96" x 110"
• 3" and 6" borders (twin & full)	6 x 12	8 x 12	8 x 12	10 x 12
• 3", 4", 5" borders (queen)	72 blocks	96 blocks	96 blocks	120 blocks
• 3", 4", 6" borders (king)				
Quilt Layout 2	72" x 96"	72" x 96"	81" x 98"	95" x 98"
• 2" and 6" borders (twin & full)	8 x 10	8 x 10	9 x 10	11 x 10
• 3" and 6" borders (queen & king)	80 blocks	80 blocks	90 blocks	110 blocks
Quilt Layout 3	57½" x 97"	77¼" x 97"	81⅛" x 100⅞"	100⅞" x 100⅞"
• 3" and 6" borders (twin & full)	4 x 8	6 x 8	7 x 9	9 x 9
• 6" border (queen & king)	32 blocks	48 blocks	63 blocks	81 blocks
Quilt Layout 4	59½" x 95⅛"	71⅜" x 95⅛"	81¼" x 105"	105" x 105"
• 2" sashing and 2" & 5" borders(twin and full)	4 x 7	5 x 7	6 x 8	8 x 8
•2" sashing and 2" & 4" borders (queen & king)	28 blocks	35 blocks	48 blocks	64 blocks

king Non-Traditional Log Cabin Quilts

...ile designing the blocks for this book, we took the con-
...t of strips (logs) sewn around a center, and used it to cre-
... many different blocks with a contemporary look. Some
...nple quilt layouts using contemporary blocks are shown
...e, **Fig 23**.

Fig 23 - Block #10

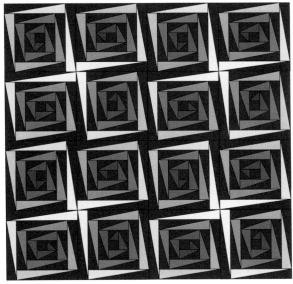

Fig 23 - Block #12

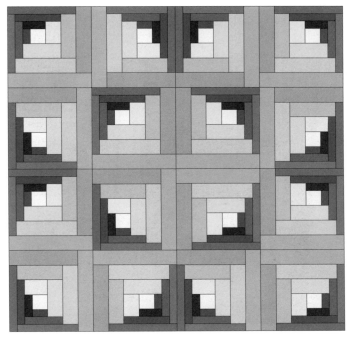

Fig 23 - Blocks #44, 45, 55 or 70

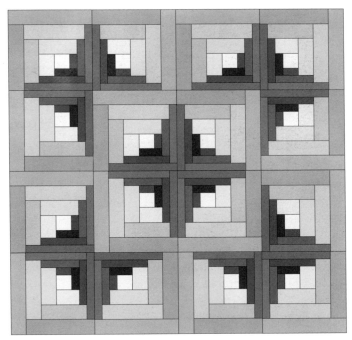

Fig 23 - Blocks #44, 45, 55 or 70

There are also several blocks that have a small block as the center square. Using these blocks together in a quilt can provide a unique quilt with a country look, **Fig 24**.

Fig 24 - Blocks 30, 61 and 87

Use the examples we've shown to plan your quilt or plan a completely different quilt. These 101 blocks are like a child's building blocks. You never know what you'll create until you start building.

Making the Quilt Top

Sew blocks (and sashing) in rows; sew rows together.

Measure quilt top lengthwise; cut two border strips to that length and sew to sides of quilt. Measure quilt top crosswise, including borders just added and cut two border strips to that length. Sew to top and bottom of quilt top. Repeat for any remaining borders.

If used, remove paper or non-woven backing at this time. **Hint:** Use a spray bottle of water to dampen paper for easier removal.

Marking the Quilting Design

Before marking on your quilt top, be sure to test any marking material to make sure it will wash out of your fabric. Mark all quilting lines on the right side of the fabric. For marking, use a hard lead pencil, chalk or other special quilt marking materials. If you quilt right on the marked lines, they will not show.

A word of caution: Marking lines which are intended to disappear after quilting—either by exposure to air or with water—may become permanent when set with a hot iron. Therefore, don't iron your quilt top after you have marked your quilting pattern.

If you are quilting around shapes, you may not need to mark the lines if you feel that you can accurately gauge the quilting line as you work. If you are quilting "in the ditch" of the seam (the space right in the seam), marking is not necessary. Any other quilting will need to be marked.

If you plan to tie your quilt, you do not need to mark it.

Attaching the Batting and Backing

There are a number of different types of batting on the market. Choose the one that is right for your quilt. Very thin cotton batting will require a great deal of quilting to hold it (quilting lines no more than 1" apart); very thick batting should be used only for tied quilts. A medium-loft bonded polyester batting is a good choice for machine quilting.

Hint: *Remove batting from its packaging a day in advance and open it out full size. This will help the batting to lie flat.*

Use 100% cotton fabric for the backing of your quilt. Bed sheets are usually not good backing materials. If you are making a bed-sized quilt, you will most likely have to piece your fabric to fit the quilt top. Cut off the selvages and sew pieces together carefully; press seams open. This is the only time i making a quilt that seams should b pressed open. Cut batting and backin about 2" larger than the quilt top on a sides. Place backing, wrong side up, a flat surface. Place batting centered c top of backing, then center quilt rig side up on batting.

The layers of the quilt must now t held together before quilting. There a three methods: thread basting, safe pin basting and quilt gun basting.

For thread basting, baste with lor stitches, starting in the center an sewing toward the edges in a number diagonal lines.

For safety pin basting, pin through a layers at once starting from the cent and working out to the edges. Place th pins no more than 4" to 6" apart. Thir of your quilt plan as you work an make certain that your pins avoid th prospective quilting lines. Choose rus proof pins that are #1 or #2. To mal pinning easier, many quilters use a qu ter's spoon. The spoon is notched s that it can push the points of the safe pins closed.

For quilt gun basting, use the hand trigger tool (found in quilt and fabr stores) that pushes nylon tags throug all layers of the quilt. Start in the cent and work randomly toward the outsid edges. Place tags about 4" apart. Yo can sew right over the tags and the they can be easily removed by cuttin off with a pair of scissors.

Quilting

Your quilt can be either machine hand quilted. **Note:** *Hand quilting m be a little more difficult if fabric or musl was used as a foundation since there is extra layer of fabric to quilt through.* you have never used a sewing machi for quilting, you might want to rea more about the technique. *Quilting f People Who Don't Have Time to Qui*

Book #4111 by Marti Michell and *A Beginner's Guide to Machine Quilting*, Book #4121 by Judi Tyrell, both published by ASN Publishing, are excellent introductions to machine quilting. These books are available at your local quilt store or department, or write the publisher for a list of sources.

You do not need a special machine for quilting. You can machine quilt with almost any home sewing machine. Just make sure that it is oiled and in good working condition. An even-feed foot is a good investment if you are going to machine quilt since it is designed to feed the top and bottom layers of the quilt through the machine evenly.

Use fine transparent nylon thread in the top and regular sewing thread in the bobbin.

To quilt in the ditch of a seam (this is actually stitching in the space between two pieces of fabric that have been sewn together), use your fingers to pull the blocks or pieces apart and machine stitch right between the two pieces. Try to keep your stitching just to the side of the seam that does not have the bulk of the seam allowance under it. When you have finished stitching, the quilting will be practically hidden in the seam.

Free form machine quilting is done with a darning foot and the feed dogs down on your sewing machine. It can be used to quilt around a design or to quilt a motif. Mark your quilting design as described in Marking the Quilting Design on page 10. Free form machine quilting takes practice to master because you are controlling the quilt through the machine rather than the machine moving the quilt. With free form machine quilting, you can quilt in any direction—up and down, side to side and even in circles without pivoting the quilt around the needle.

Attaching the Binding

Place the quilt on a flat surface and carefully trim the backing and batting 1/2" beyond the quilt top edge. Measure the quilt top and cut two 2 1/2"-wide binding strips the length of your quilt (for sides). Fold strips in half lengthwise wrong sides together. Place one strip along one side of the quilt; sew with a 1/4" seam allowance, **Fig 25**. (Seam allowance should be measured from outer edge of quilt top fabric, not outer edge of batting/backing.)

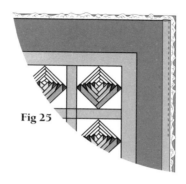

Fig 25

Turn binding to back and slipstitch to backing covering previous stitching line, **Fig 26**. Repeat on other side.

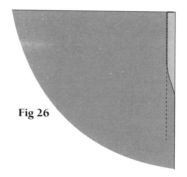

Fig 26

For top and bottom edges, measure quilt crosswise and cut two 2 1/2"-wide strips that size, adding 1/2" to each end. Fold strips in half lengthwise with wrong sides together. Place one strip along top edge with 1/2" extending beyond each side; sew with a 1/4" seam allowance, **Fig 27**. Turn binding to back and tuck the extra 1/2" under at each end; slipstitch to backing fabric.

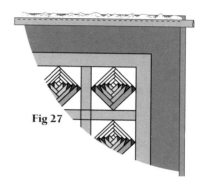

Fig 27

The Finishing Touch

When your quilt is finished, always sign and date it. A label can be cross stitched, embroidered or even written with a permanent marking pen. Hand stitch to back of quilt.

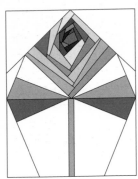

1 Crazy Rose

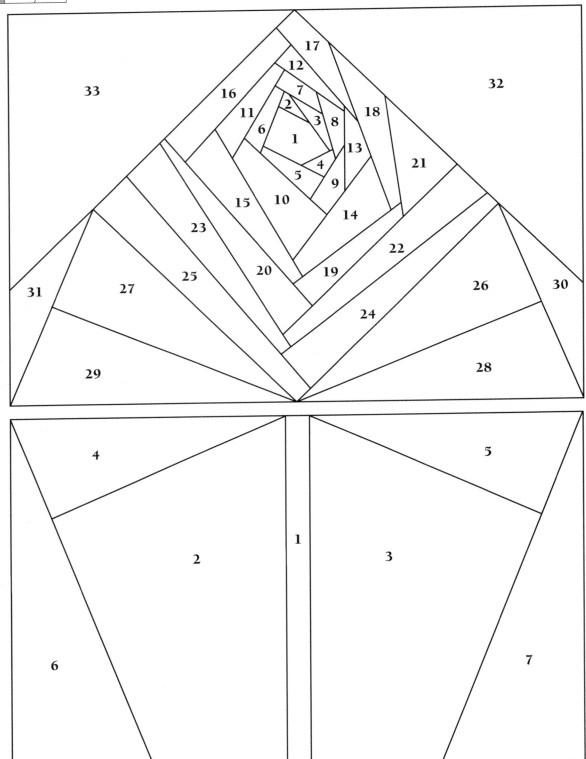

2 Sunburst

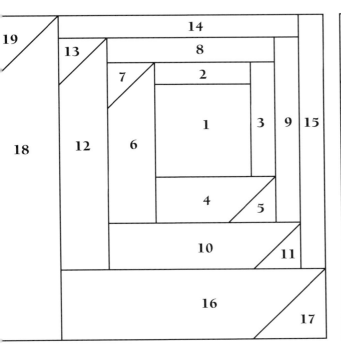

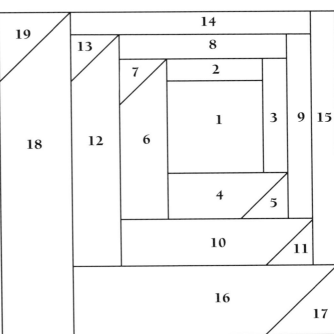

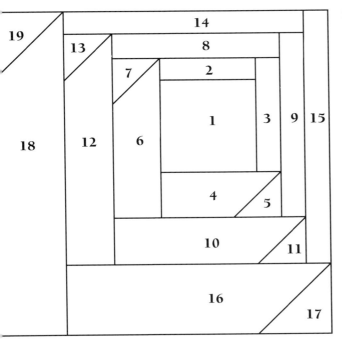

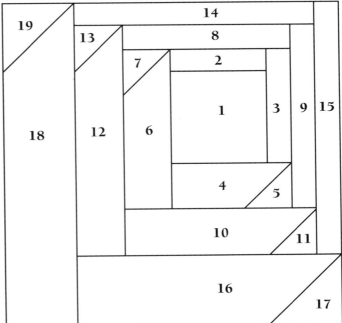

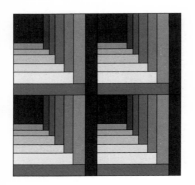

3 Log Cabin Windows

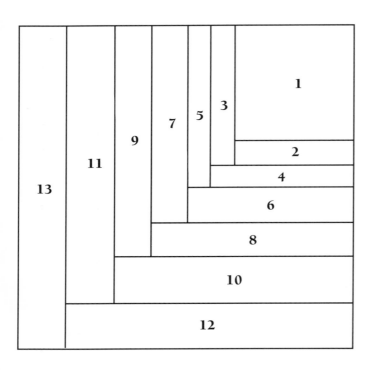

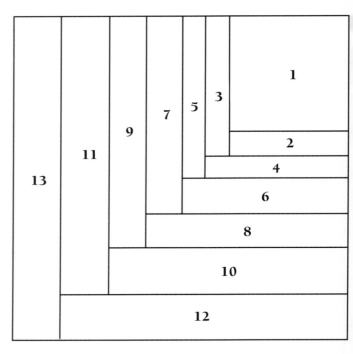

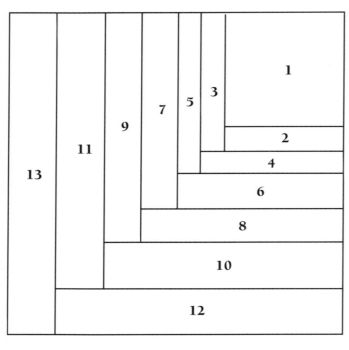

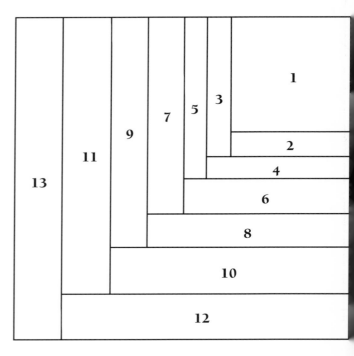

4 *Wreath in the Cabin*

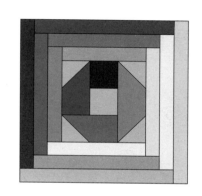

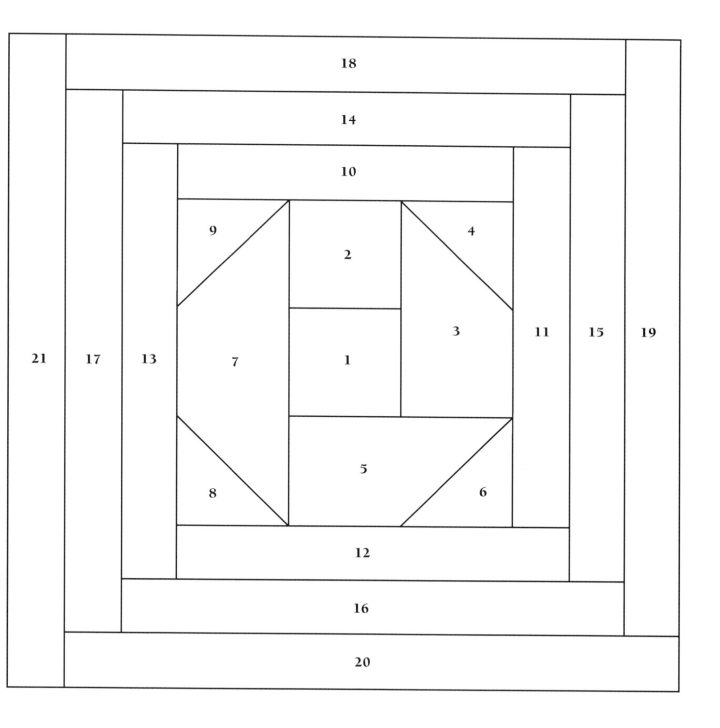

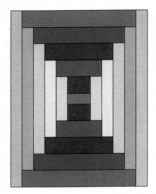

Hourglass

18

14

10

6

2

20	16	12	8	4	1	5	9	13	17	21

3

7

11

15

19

6 Dream House

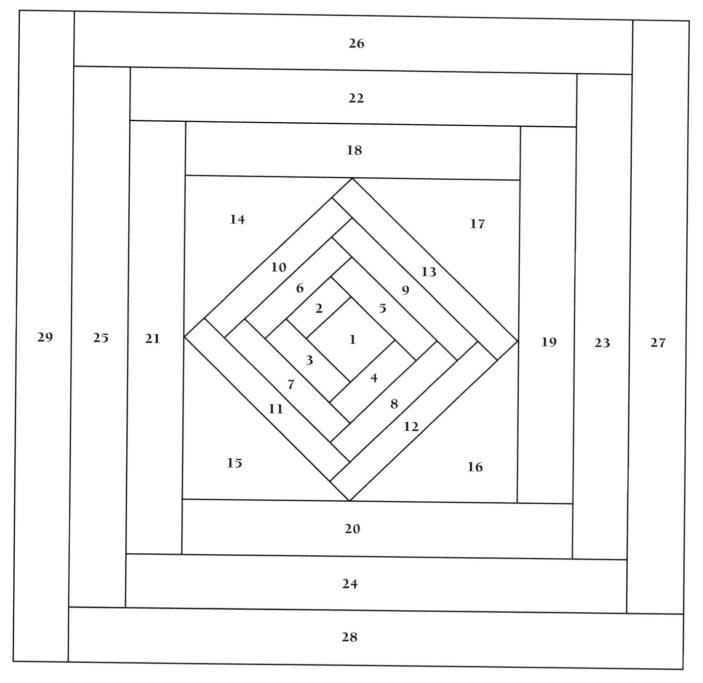

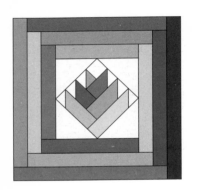

Cabin with a Garden

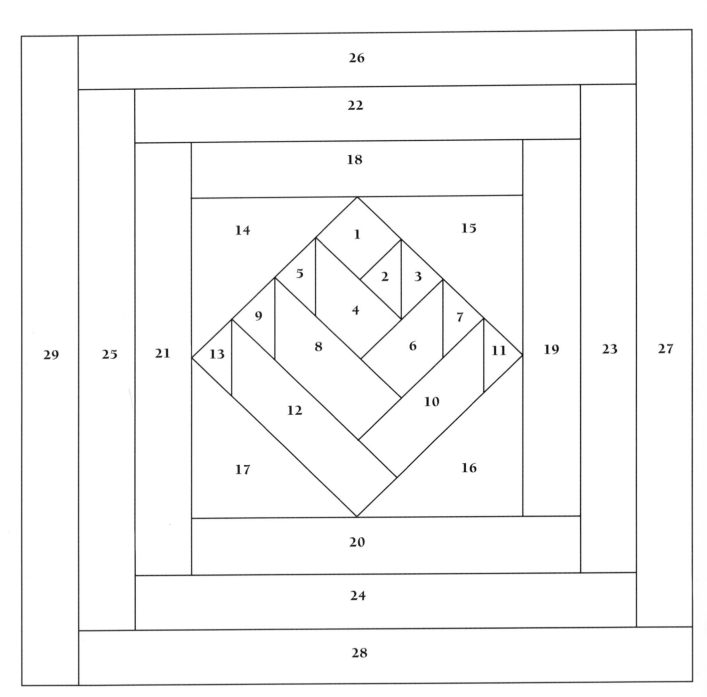

Kaleidoscope

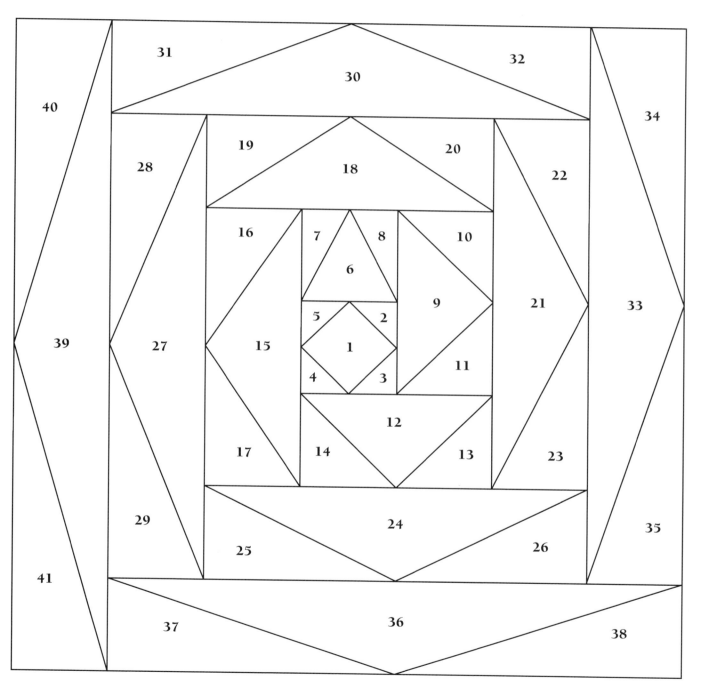

9 Medium Pineapple

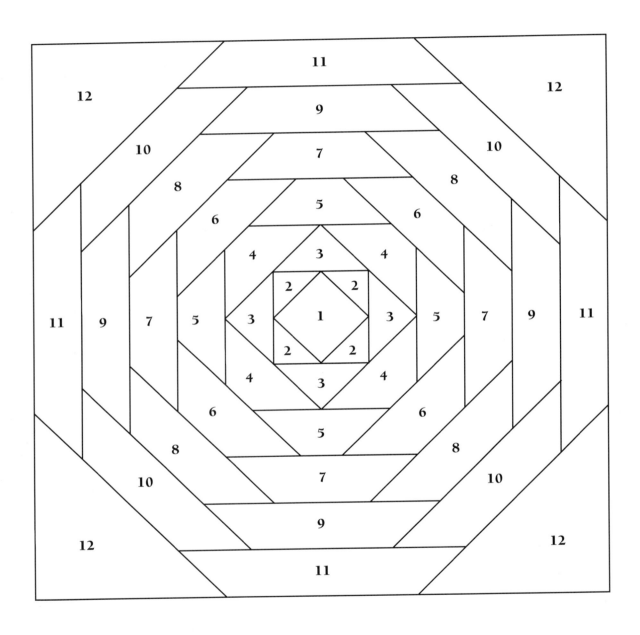

10 Dorothy's Cabin

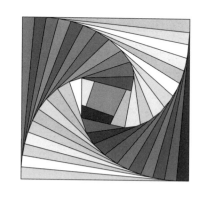

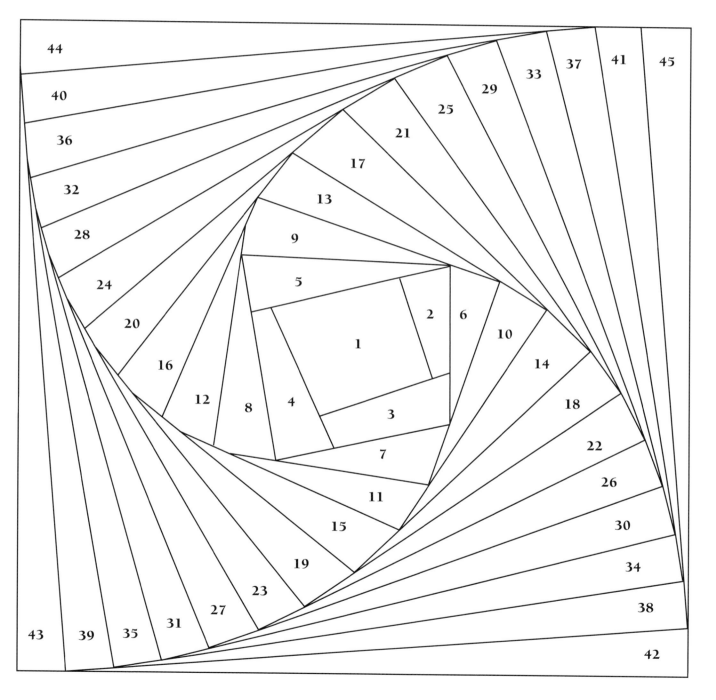

11 Pineapple Prism

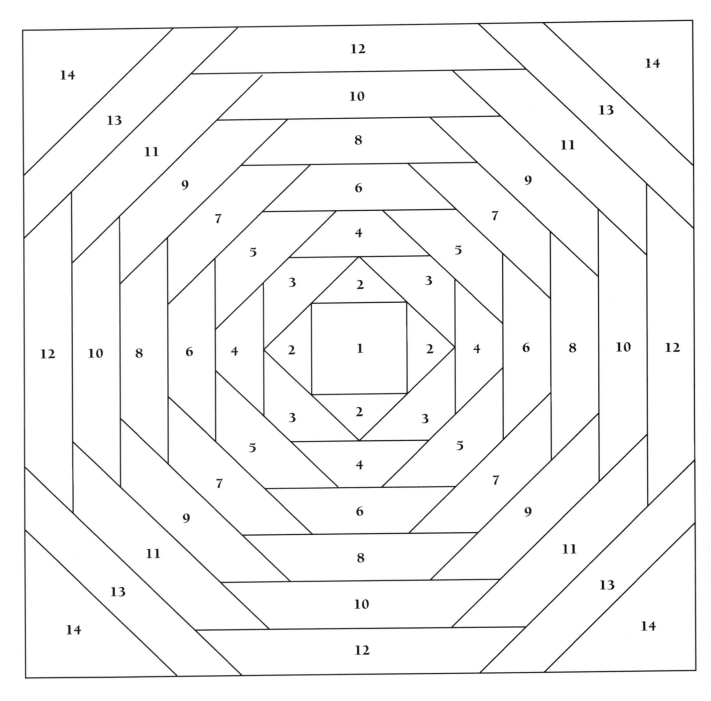

12 *Twirling Ribbon*

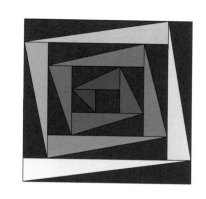

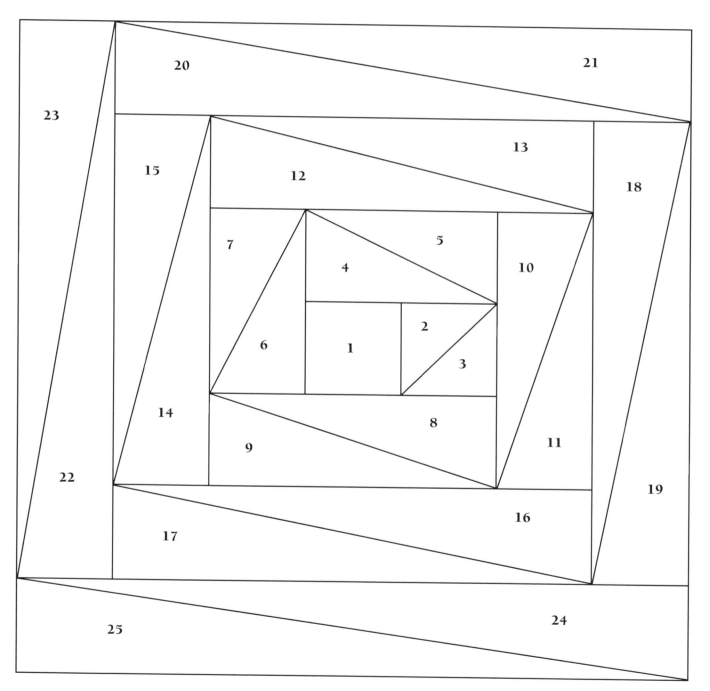

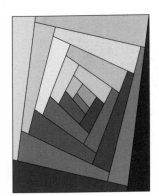

13 Log Cabin Mudslide

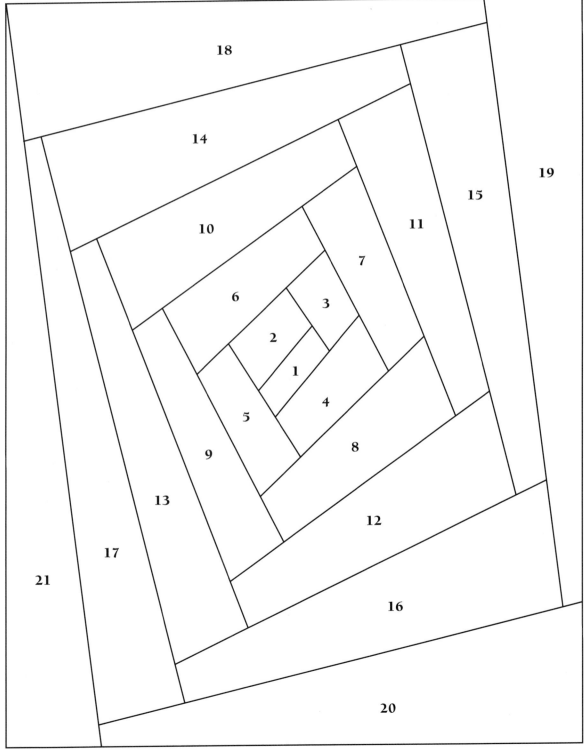

14 Birdhouse Pentagon

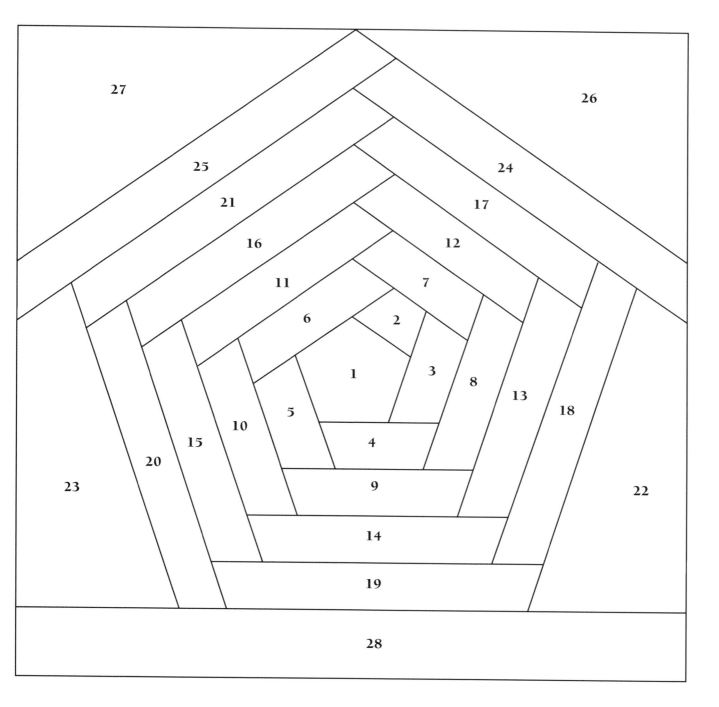

15 Vertigo

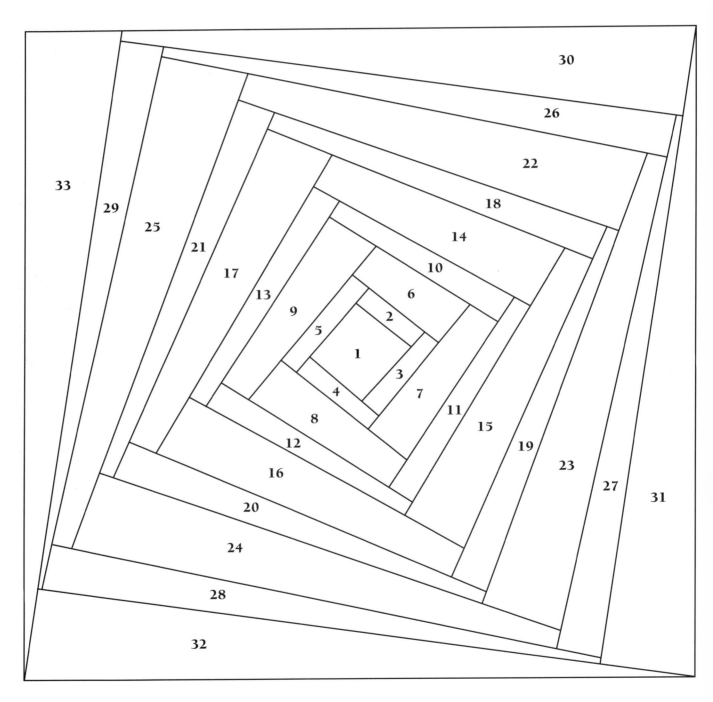

16 Sweetheart Log Cabin

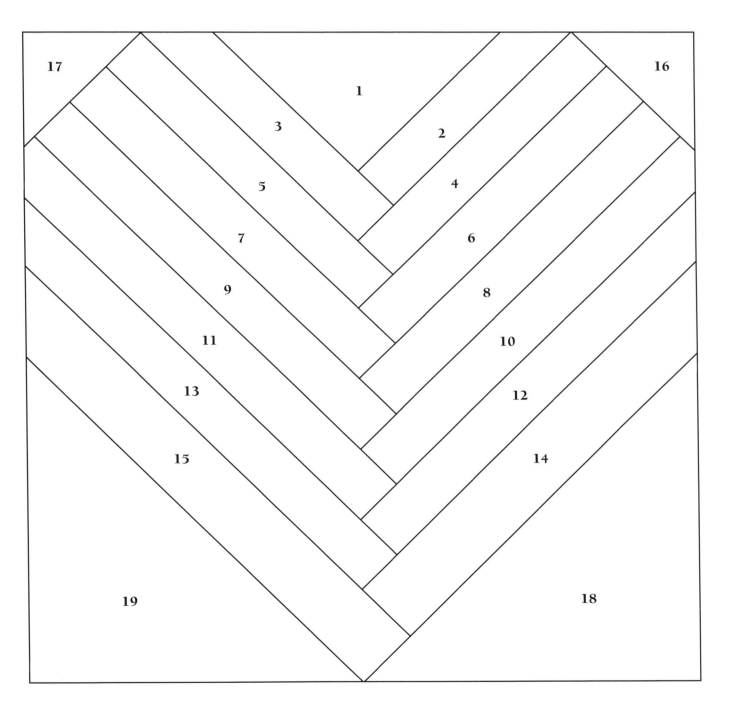

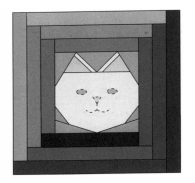

17 Cat in the Cabin

Photographed block note: *The cat's face was hand embroidered with three strands of embroidery floss as follows: eyes with green, nose with pink and mouth with dark gray.*

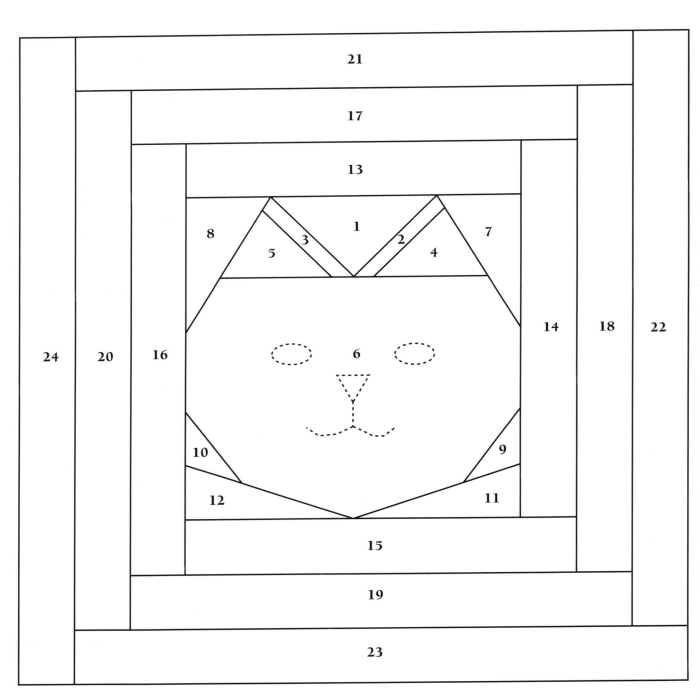

18 Bird in Flight

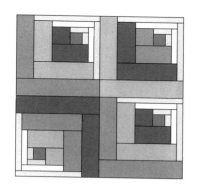

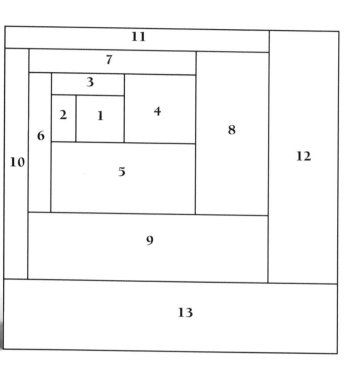

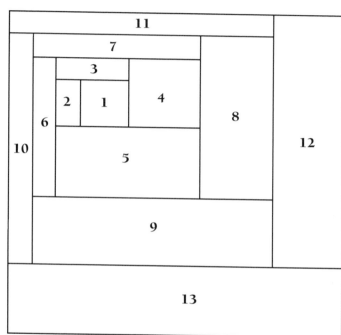

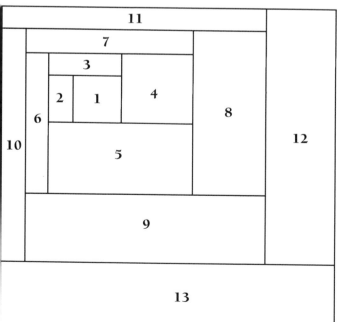

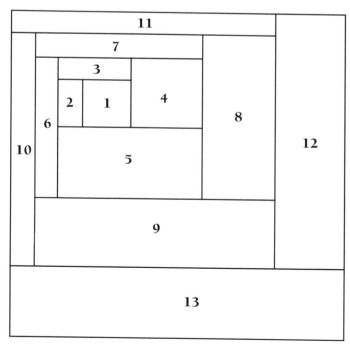

19 Bunny in the Cabin

Photographed block note: *The bunny's face was hand embroidered with three strands of embroidery floss as follows: eyes with dark gray and nose with pink.*

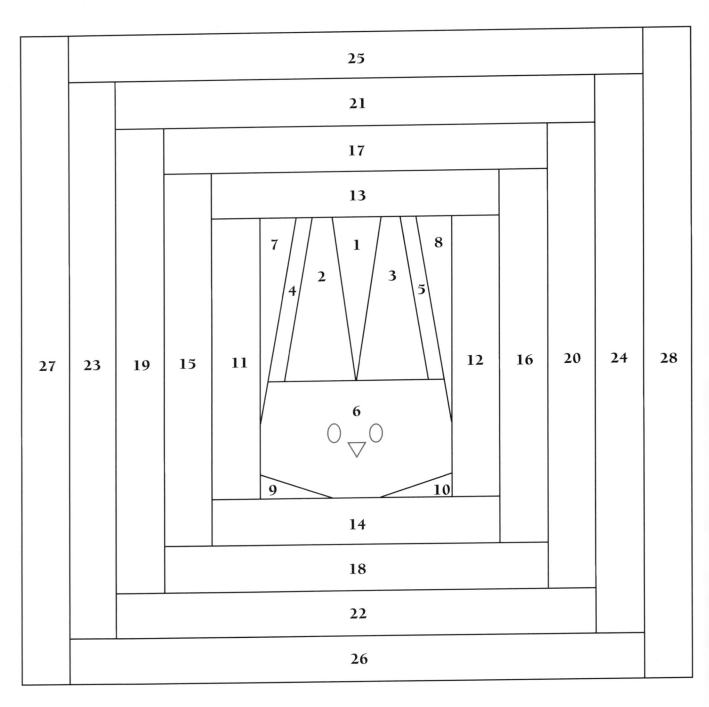

20 Diamond

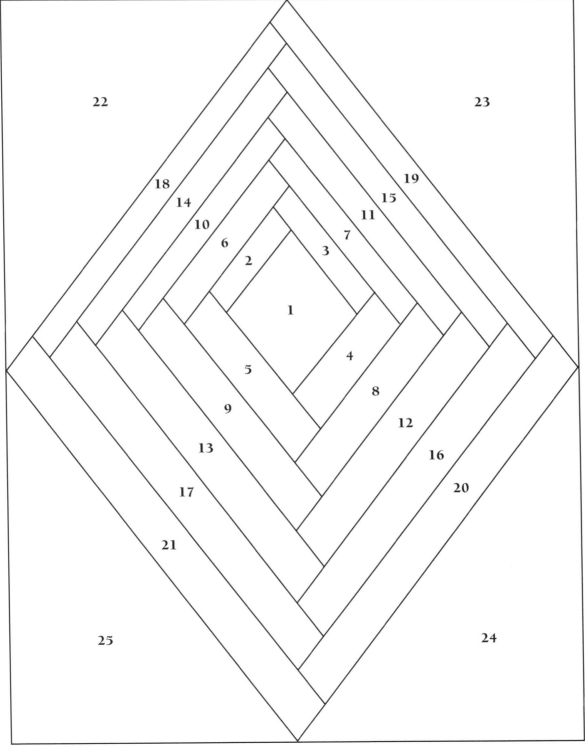

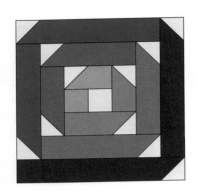

21 Rolling Logs

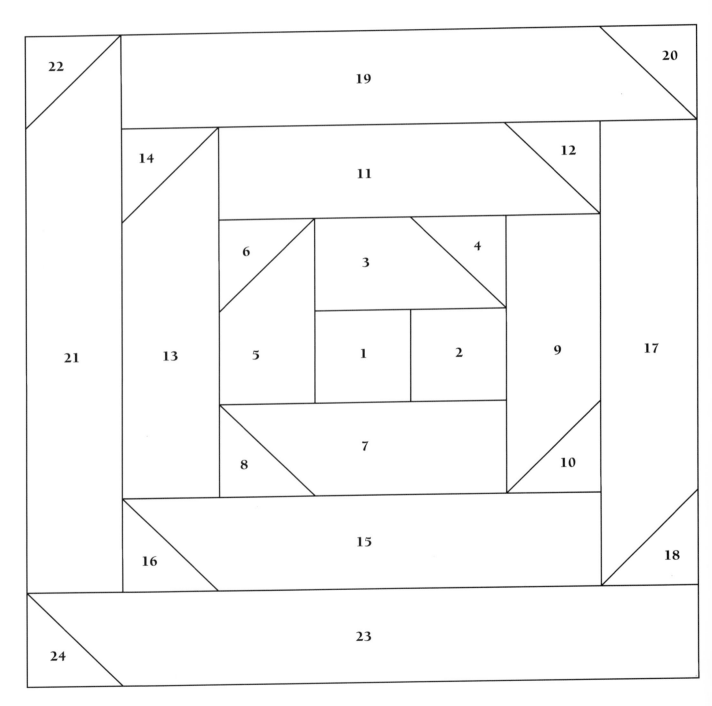

22 Thick-and-Thin

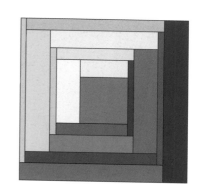

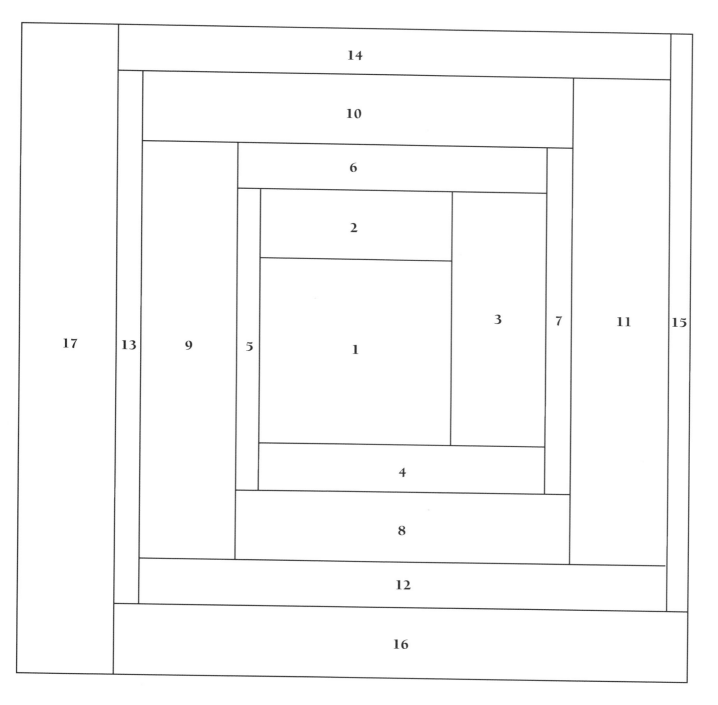

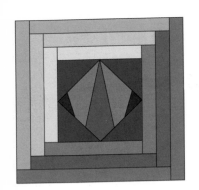

23 ✦ Splitting Headache

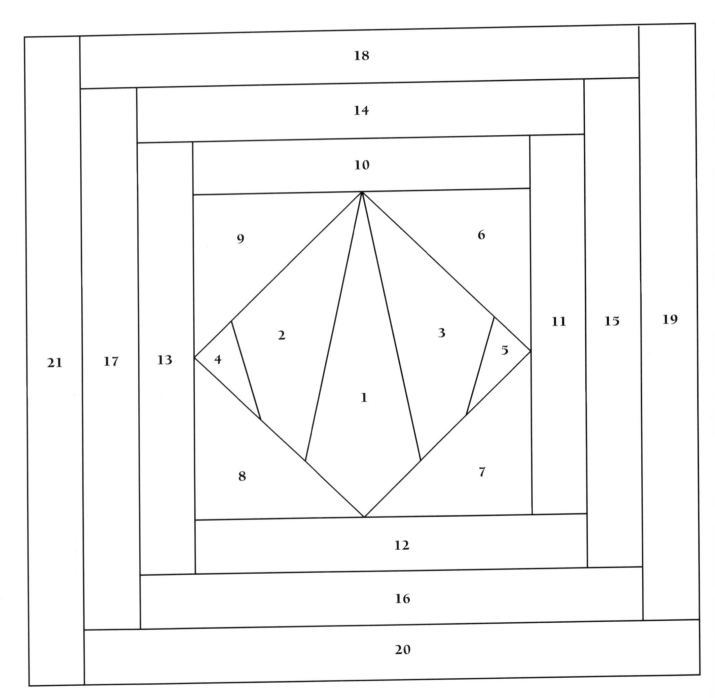

18

14

10

9   6

11   15   19

2

3

21   17   13   4   5

1

8   7

12

16

20

24 Brilliant Rose

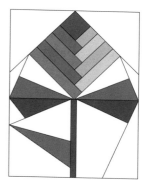

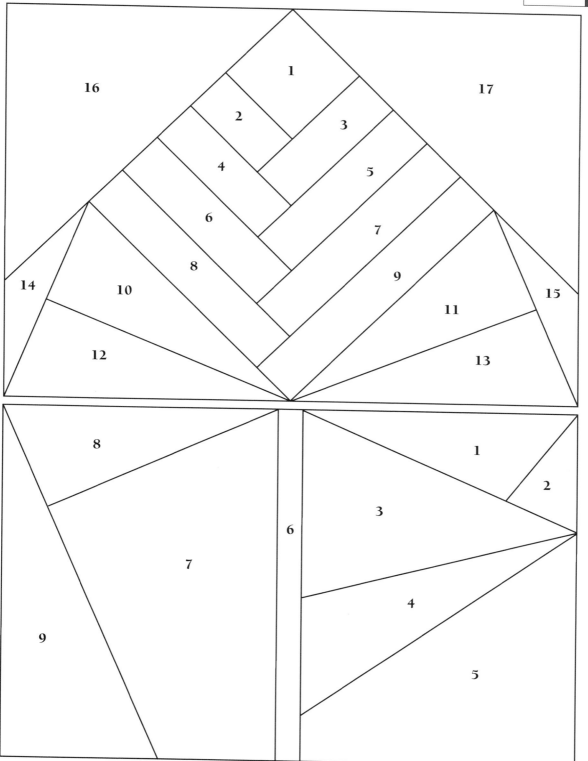

16

1

17

2

3

4

5

6

7

8

9

14

10

15

11

12

13

8

1

2

3

6

7

4

9

5

25 Slanted View

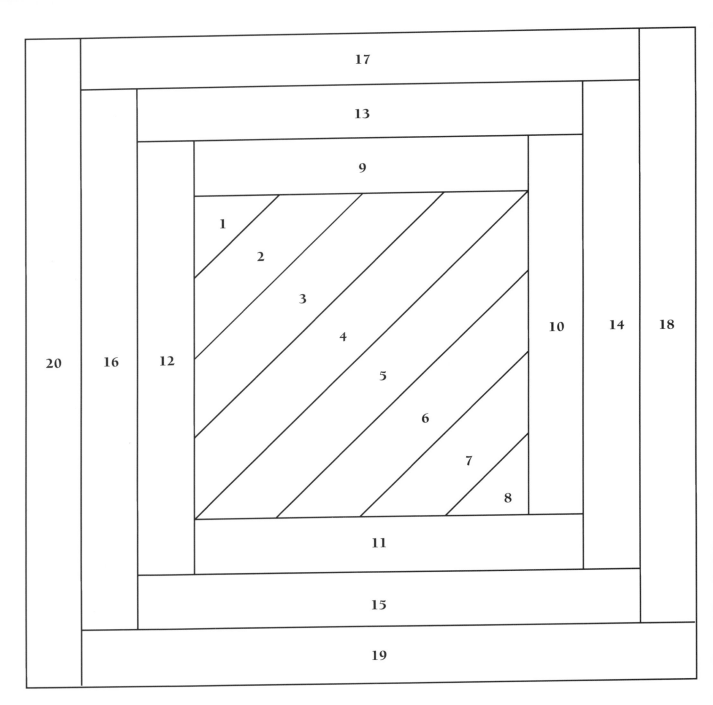

26 Rectangle Pineapple

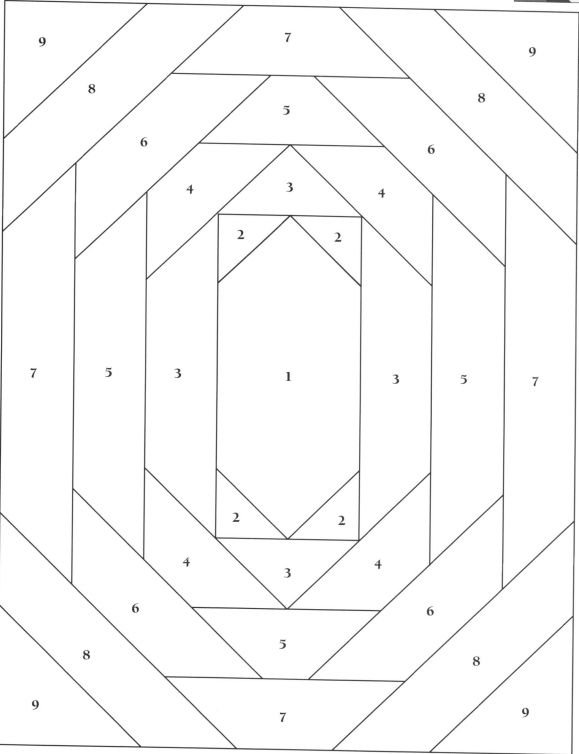

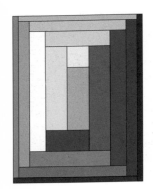

27 *Perfectly Uneven Rectangle*

14

10

6

2

1

3

5

7

9

11

13

15

17

4

8

12

16

28 Twisting Cabin in a Cabin

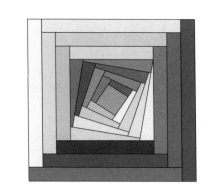

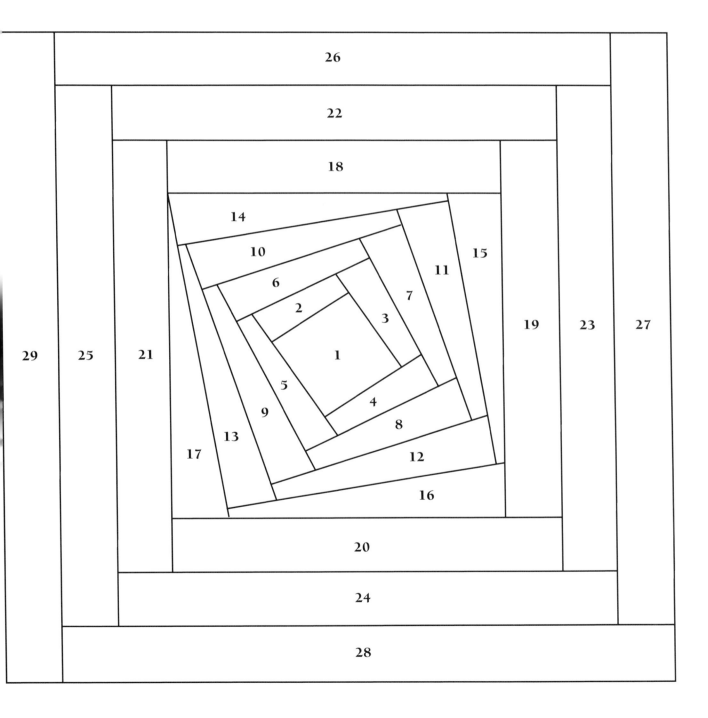

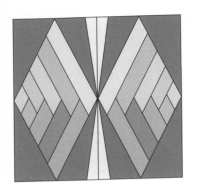

29 Sparkling Butterfly

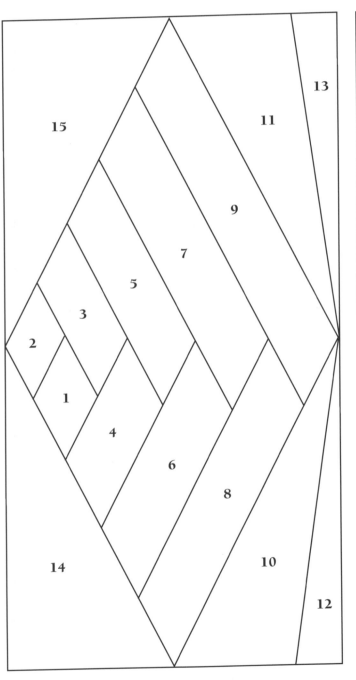

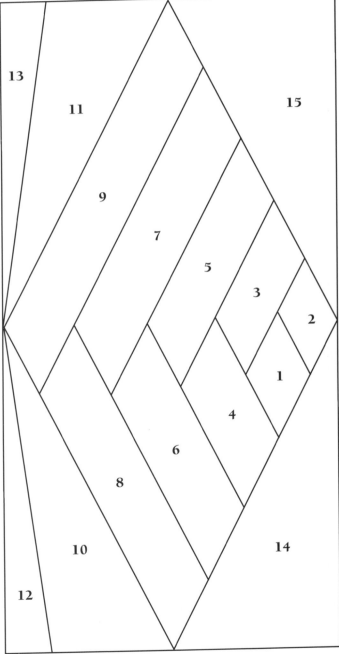

30 Pine Tree in a Cabin

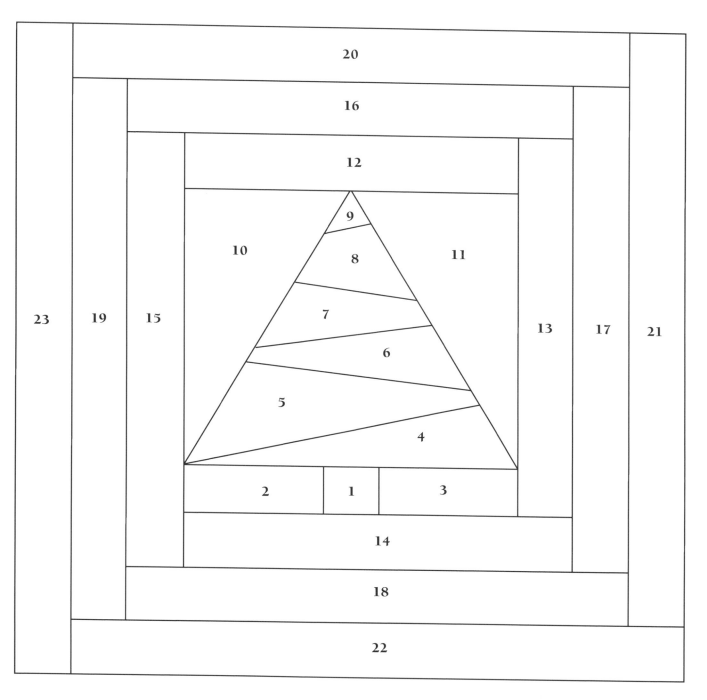

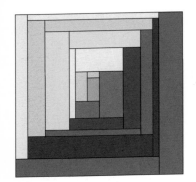

31 Wide-and-Narrow

					18					
				14					
			10					
			6				
		2				
21	17	13	9	5	1	3	7	11	15	19
			4				
		8				
		12				
		16				
		20				

32 *Five Hills in the Cabin*

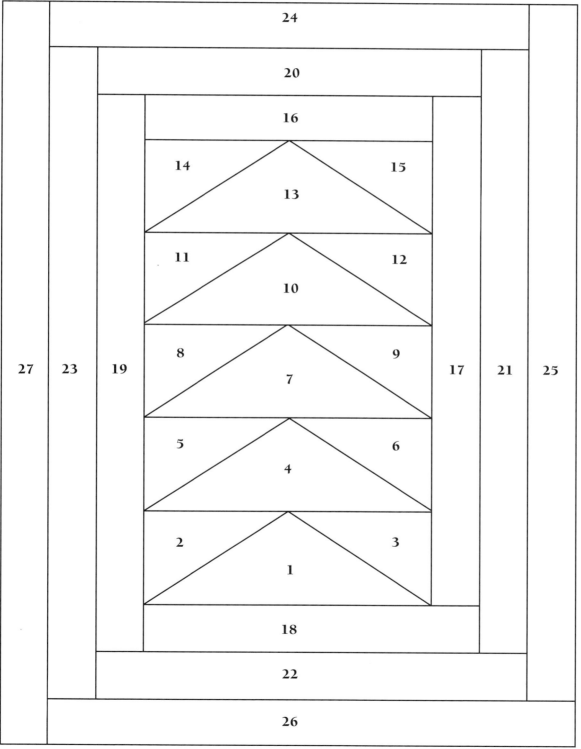

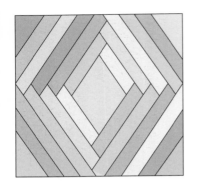

33 Iridescent Diamond

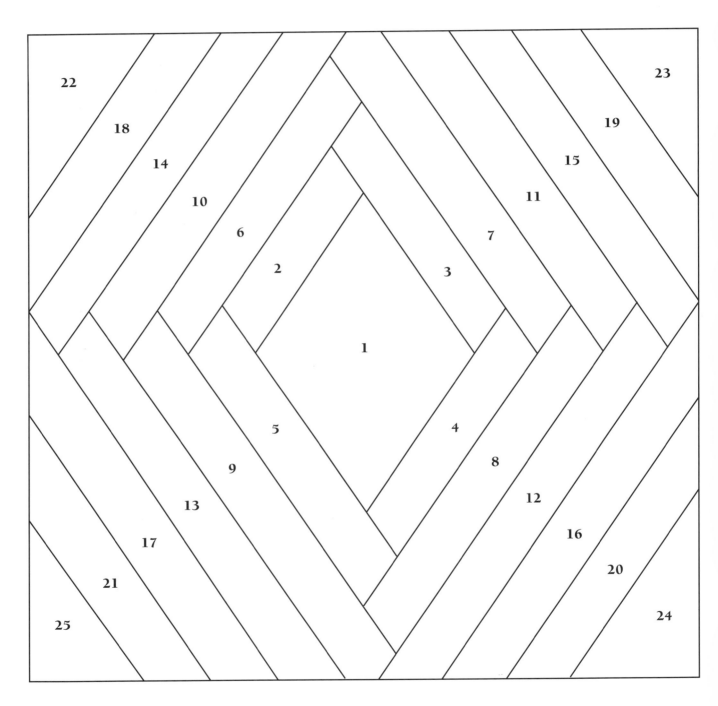

34 Half a Pineapple

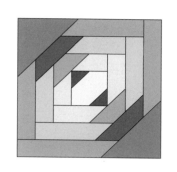

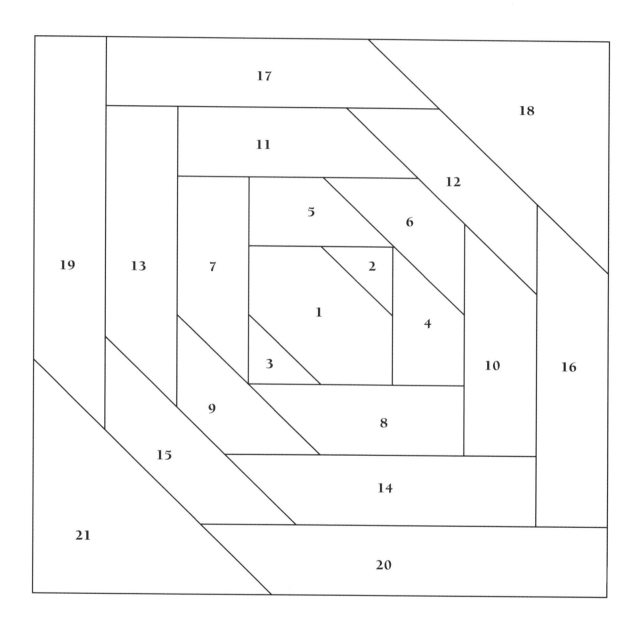

35 Through the Cabin Door

16

12

8

4

17   13   9   5   1   3   7   11   15

2

6

10

14

36 Courthouse Corners

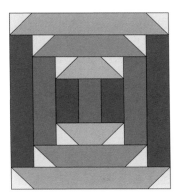

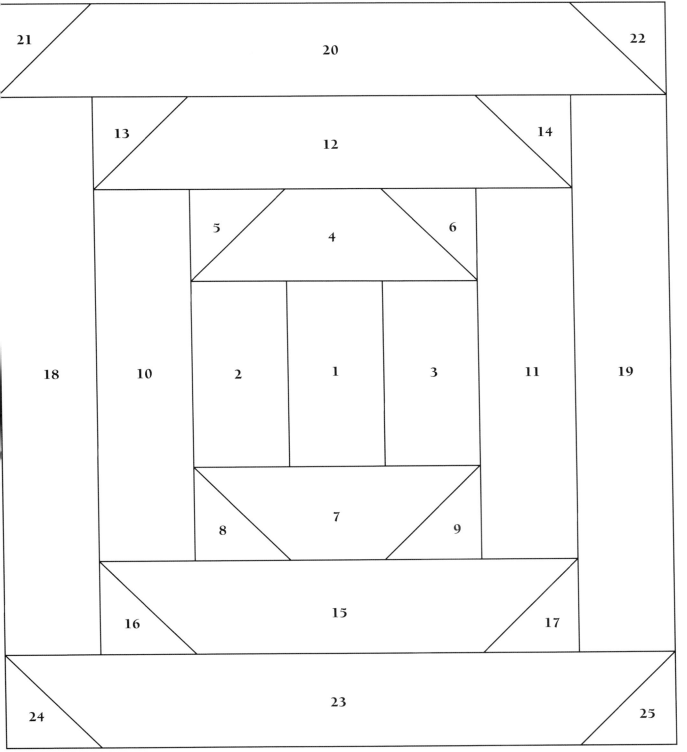

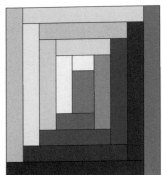

37 Tall Log Cabin

14

10

6

2

3   7   11   15

17   13   9   5   1

4

8

12

16

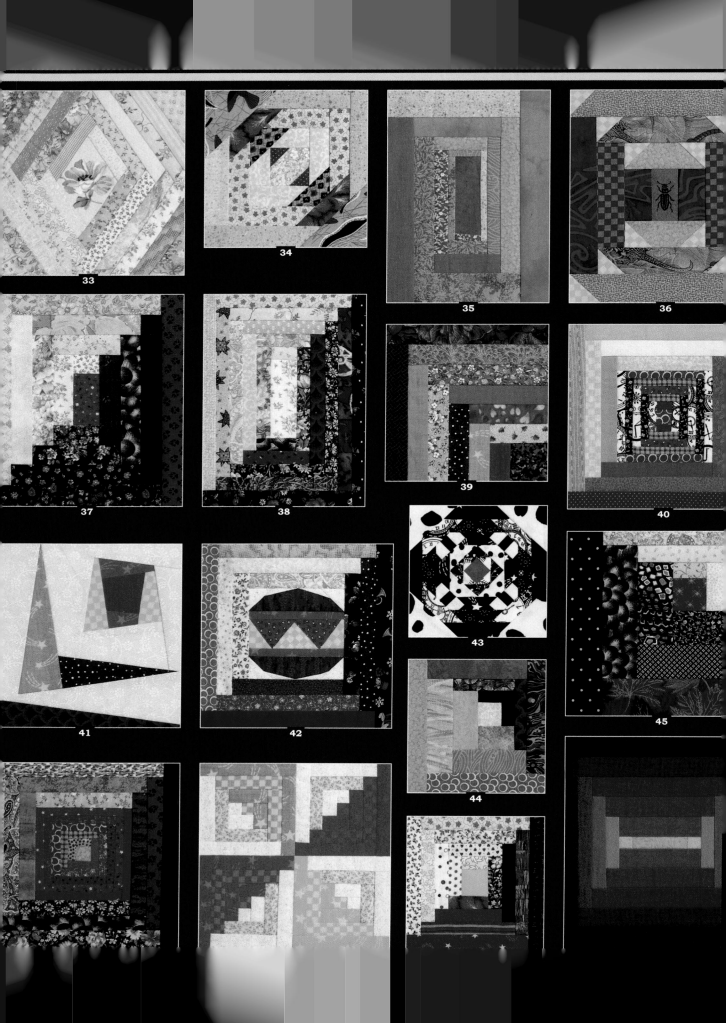

33

34

35

36

37

38

39

40

41

42

43

44

45

Log Cabin Blocks 50 - 66

50
51
52
53
54
55
56
57
58
59
60
61
62
63
64
65
66

67

68

69

70

71

72

73

74

75

76

77

78

79

80

81

82

83

38 Urban Log Cabin

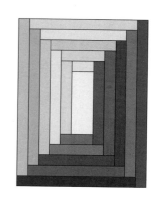

18

14

10

6

2

| 21 | 17 | 13 | 9 | 5 | 1 | 3 | 7 | 11 | 15 | 19 |

4

8

12

16

20

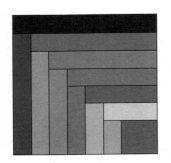

39 Medium Center in the Corn

| 13 |
| 11 |
| 9 |
| 7 |
| 5 |
| 3 |
| 1 | 2 | 4 | 6 | 8 | 10 | 12 |

40 Courthouse Steps in a Cabin

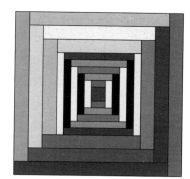

								30									
							26										
						22											
						18											
						14											
						10											
						6											
						2											
33	29	25	20	16	12	8	4	1	5	9	13	17	21	23	27	31
						3											
						7											
						11											
						15											
						19											
						24											
						28											
						32											

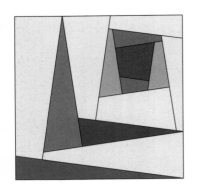

41 Abstract Flower

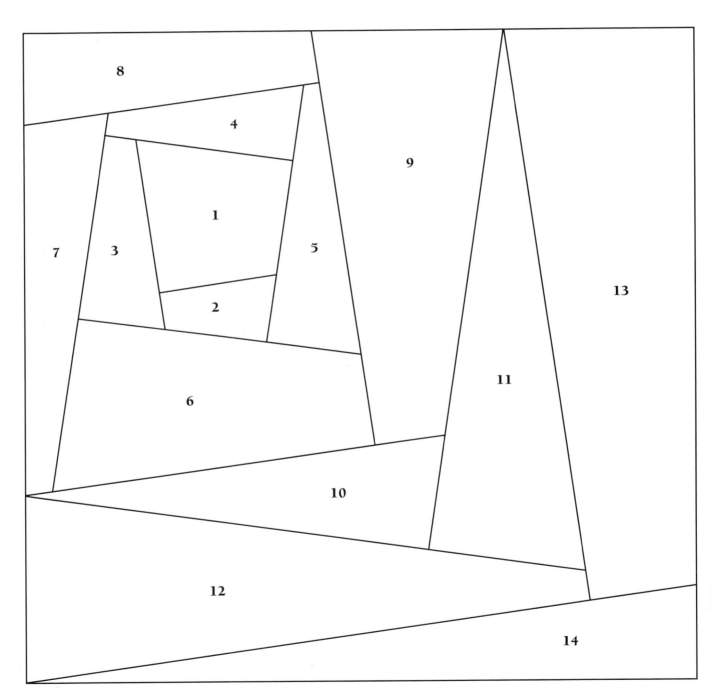

 **42 Ornament in a Cabin**

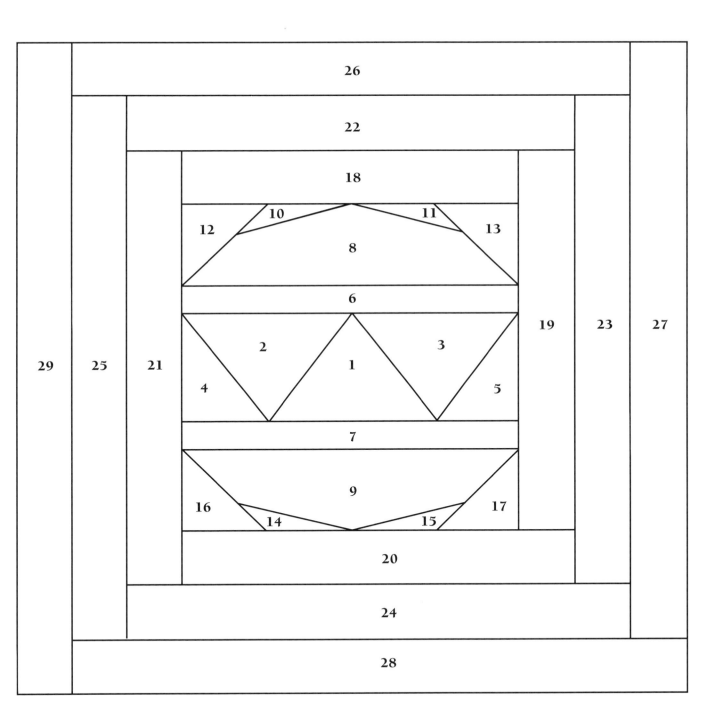

43 Small Pineapple

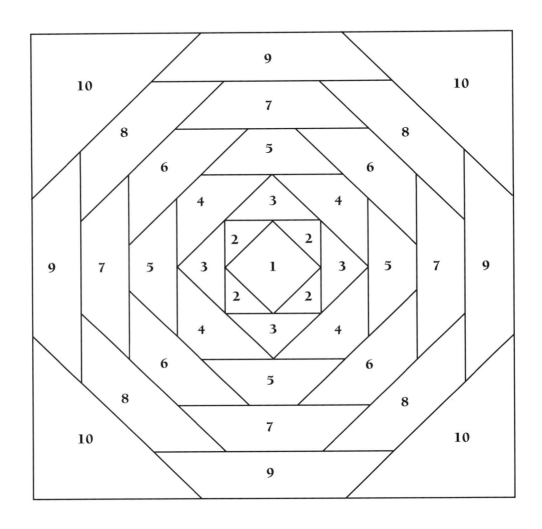

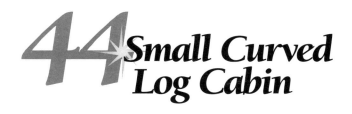

44 Small Curved Log Cabin

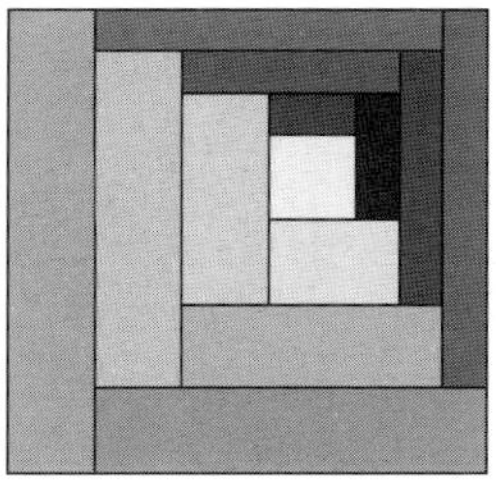

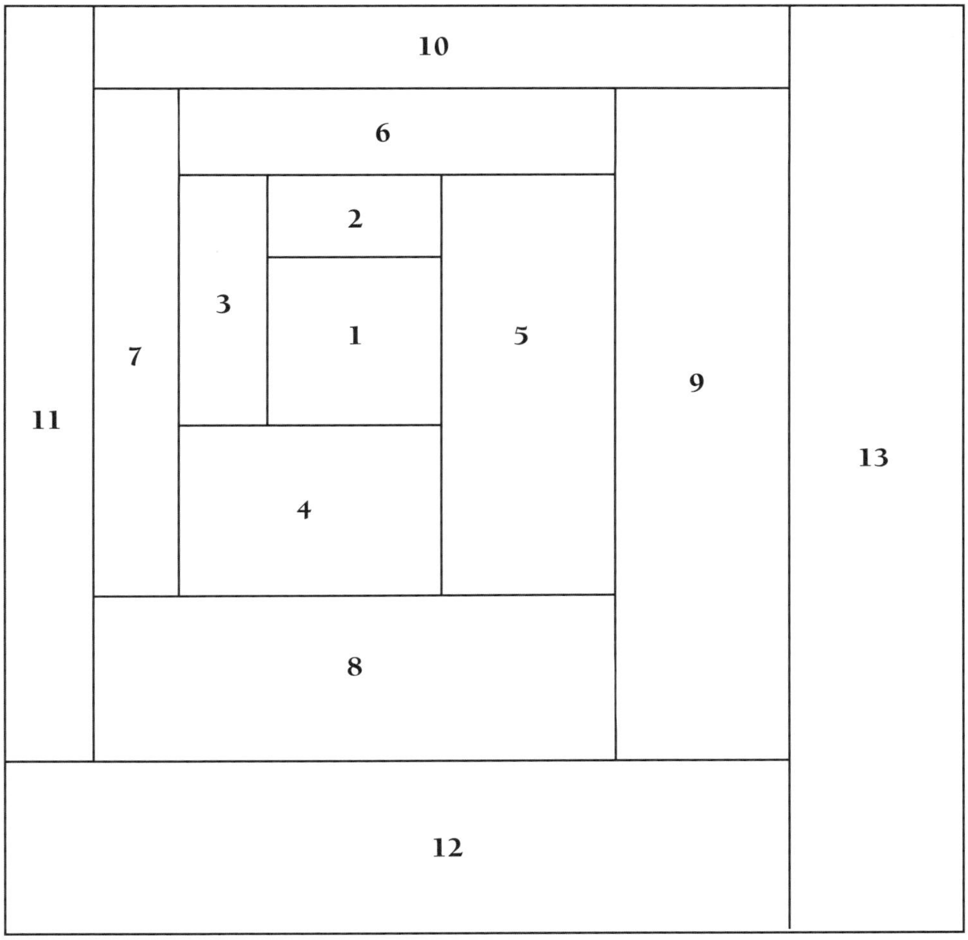
10
6
2
3
1
5
7
9
11
13
4
8
12

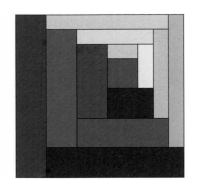

45 Large Curved Log Cabin

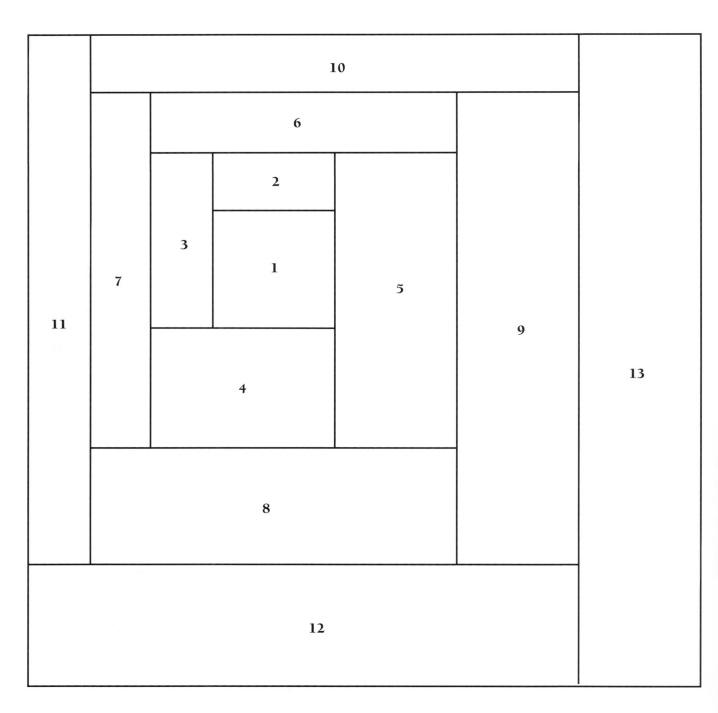

 **Log Cabin in a Cabin**

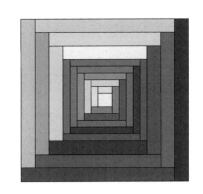

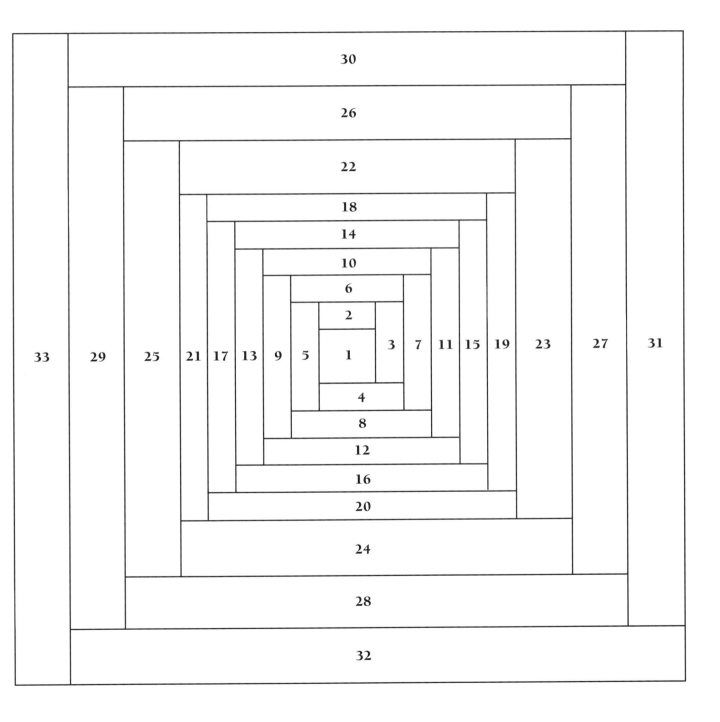

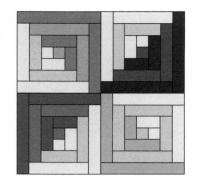

47 Log Cabin Pinwheel

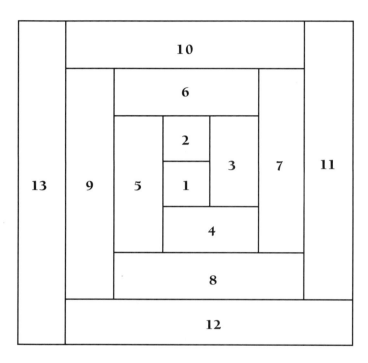

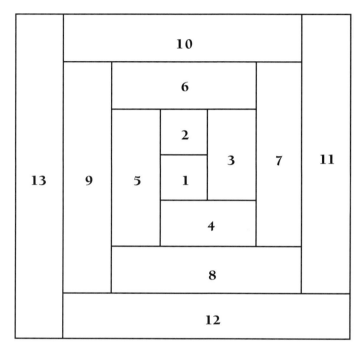

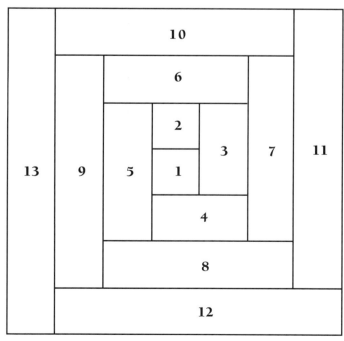

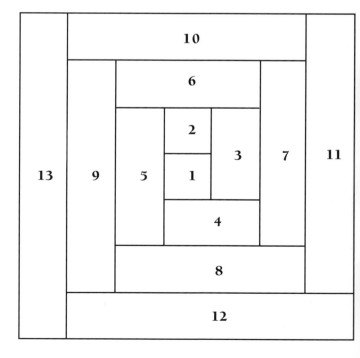

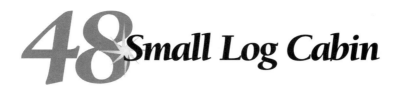

48 Small Log Cabin

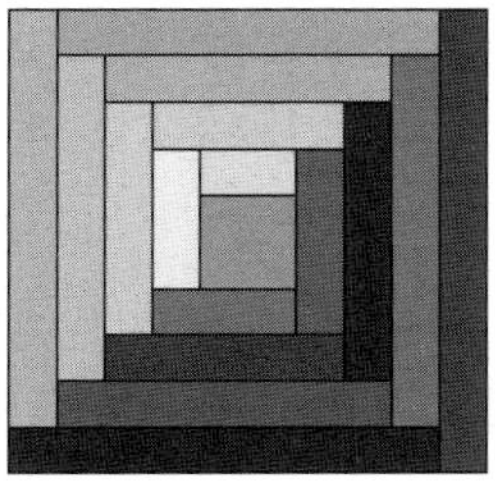

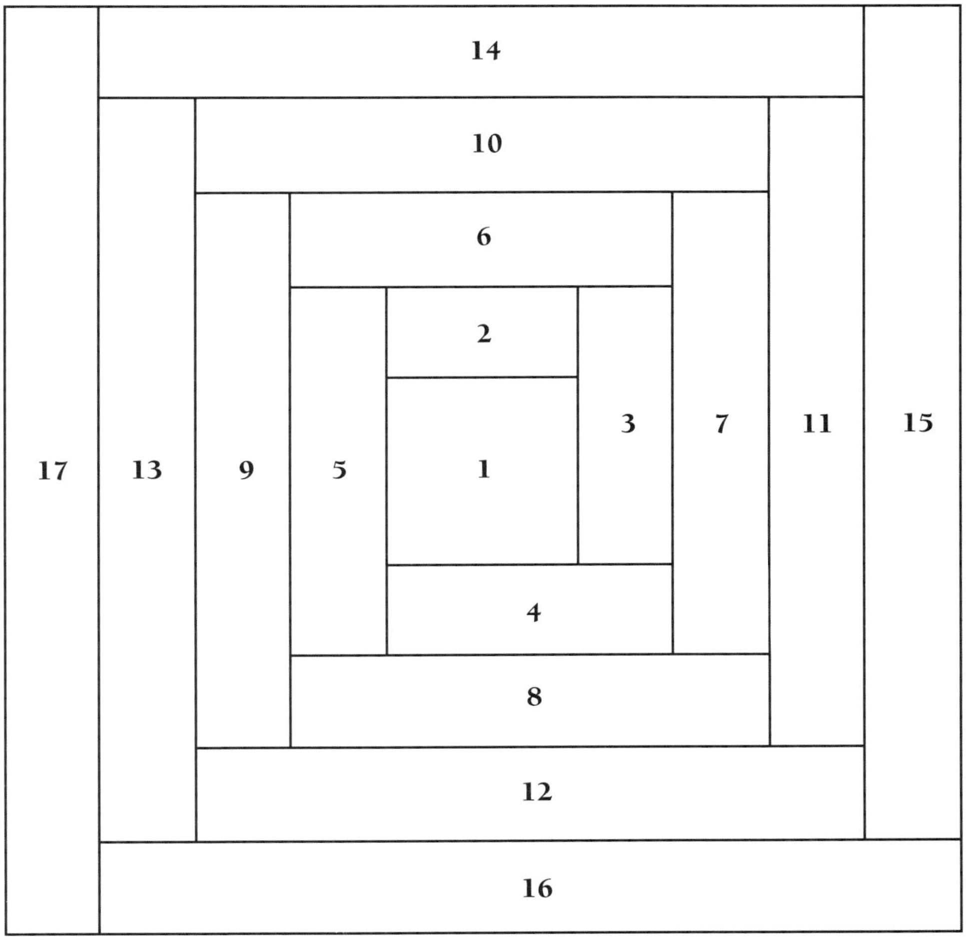
14
10
6
2
17
13
9
5
1
3
7
11
15
4
8
12
16

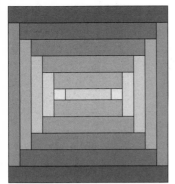

49 Cathedral Steps

						20							
						16							
						12							
						8							
						4							
18	14	10	6	2		1		3	7	11	15	19
						5							
						9							
						13							
						17							
						21							

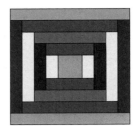

					16					
					12					
					8					
					4					
14	10	6	2		1		3	7	11	15
					5					
					9					
					13					
					17					

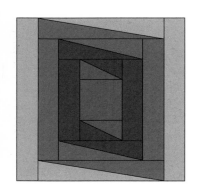

51 Skewed Window

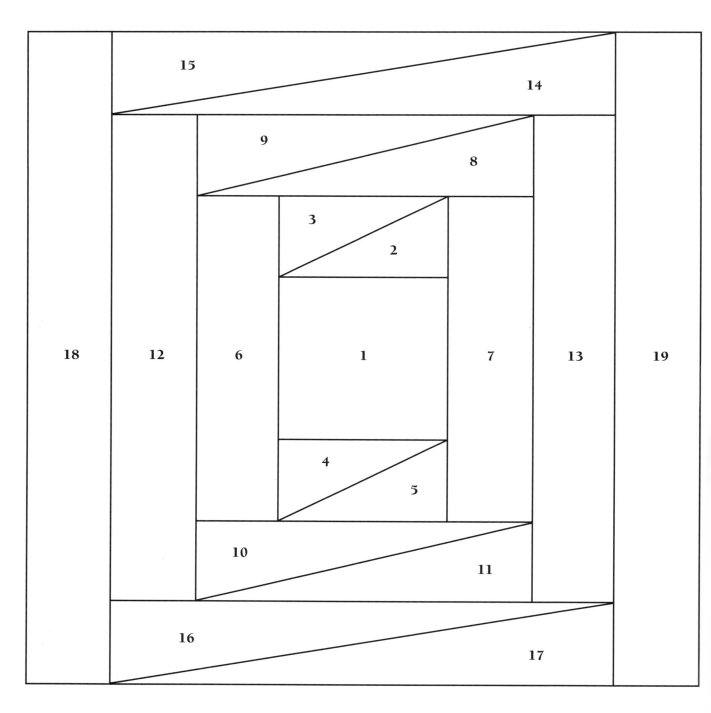

52 Log A-Frame

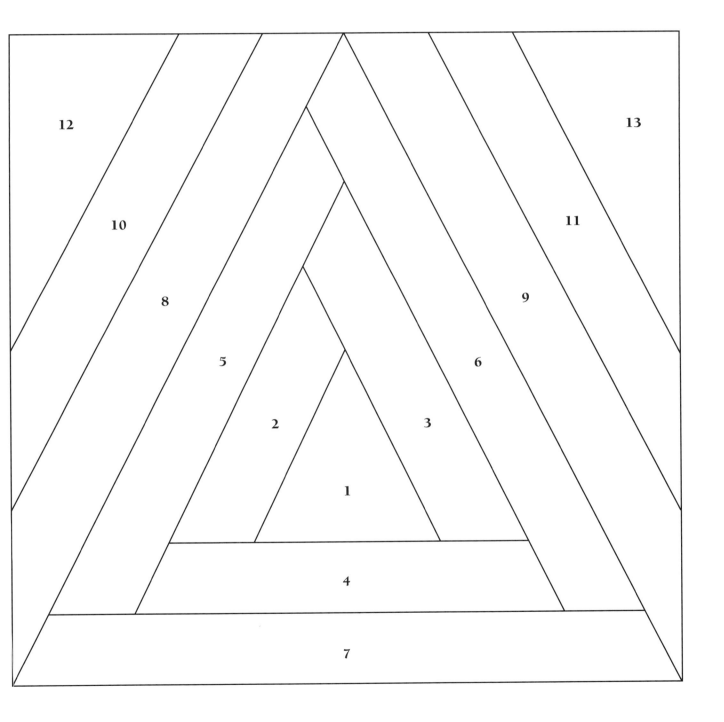

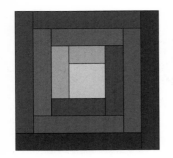

53 Medium Log Cabin

						10					
				6					
				2					
13	9	5		1		3	7	11
				4					
				8					
				12					

 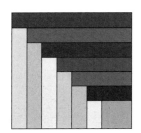

54 Small Center in the Corner

```
┌─────────────────────────────────────────┐
│                    13                     │
├──────────────────────────────────┬───────┤
│                 11               │       │
├────────────────────────────┬─────┤       │
│              9             │     │       │
├──────────────────────┬─────┤     │  12   │
│           7          │    │     │       │
├──────────────┬───────┤    │ 10  │       │
│       5      │      │ 8  │     │       │
├──────┬───────┤  6   │    │     │       │
│   3  │      │     │    │     │       │
├──────┼───────┤    │    │     │       │
│      │      │ 4  │    │     │       │
│  1   │  2   │    │    │     │       │
└──────┴──────┴────┴────┴─────┴───────┘
```

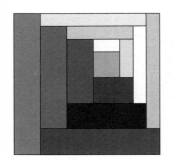

55 Medium Curved Log Cabin

56 Spinning Log Cabin

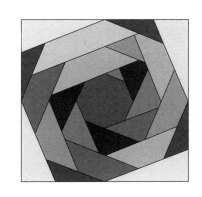

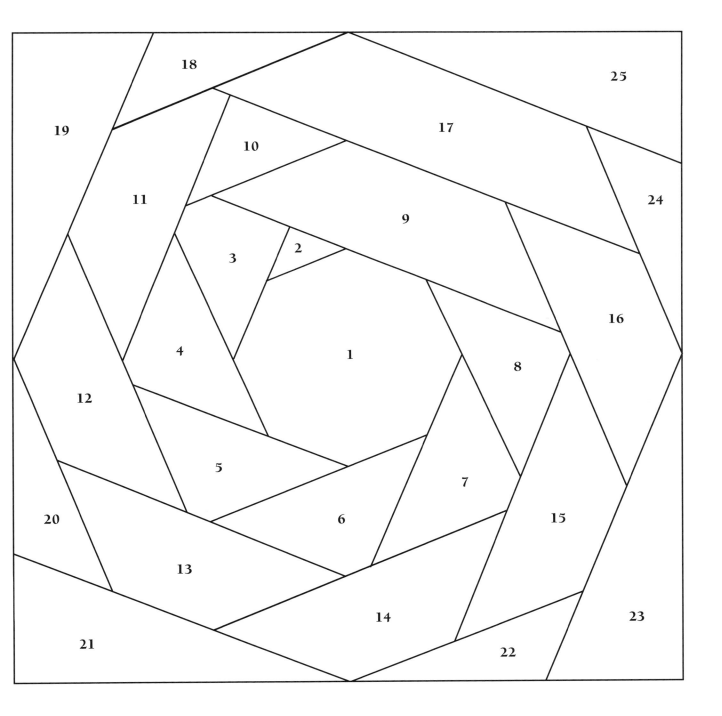

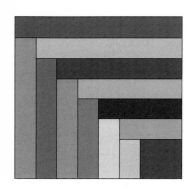

57 Large Center in the Corner

13

11

9

7

5

3

1

2

4

6

8

10

12

58 Diamond in the Cabin

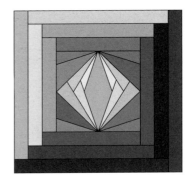

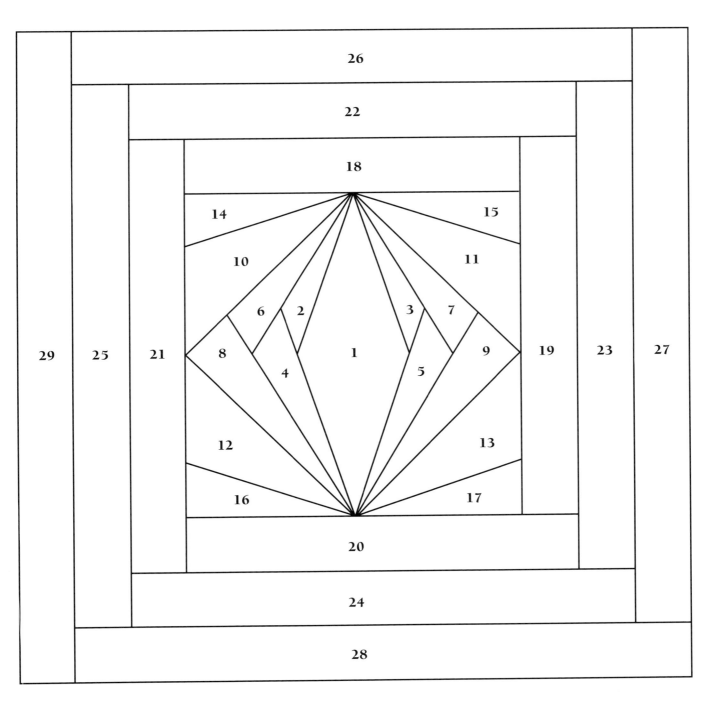

26

22

18

14   15

10   11

6 2   3 7

8   9

1

4   5

21   19   23   27

29   25

12   13

16   17

20

24

28

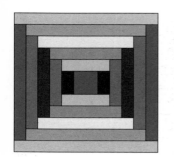

59 Medium Courthouse Steps

									20										

16

12

8

4

18 14 10 6 2 1 3 7 11 15 19

5

9

13

17

21

74

60 Pineapple in the Cabin

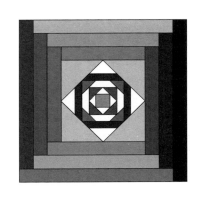

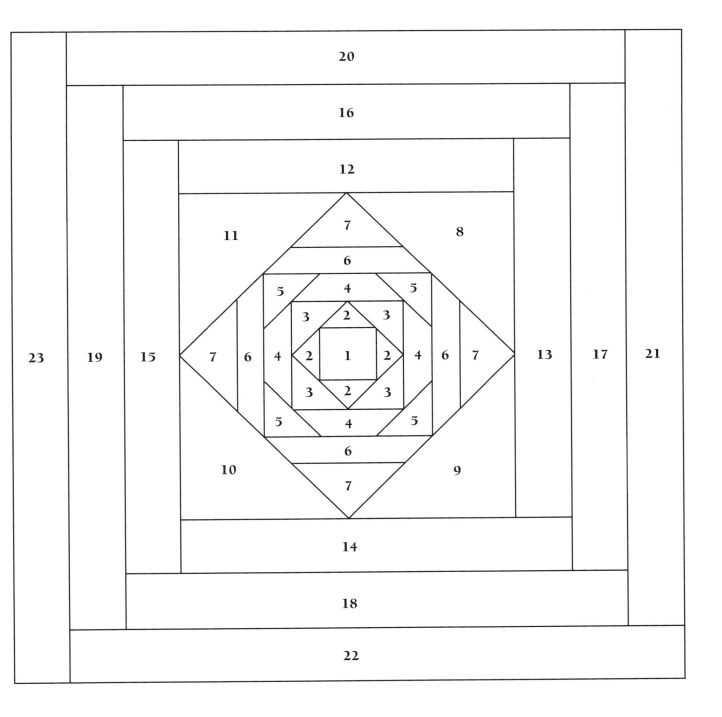

61 Heart of the Cabin

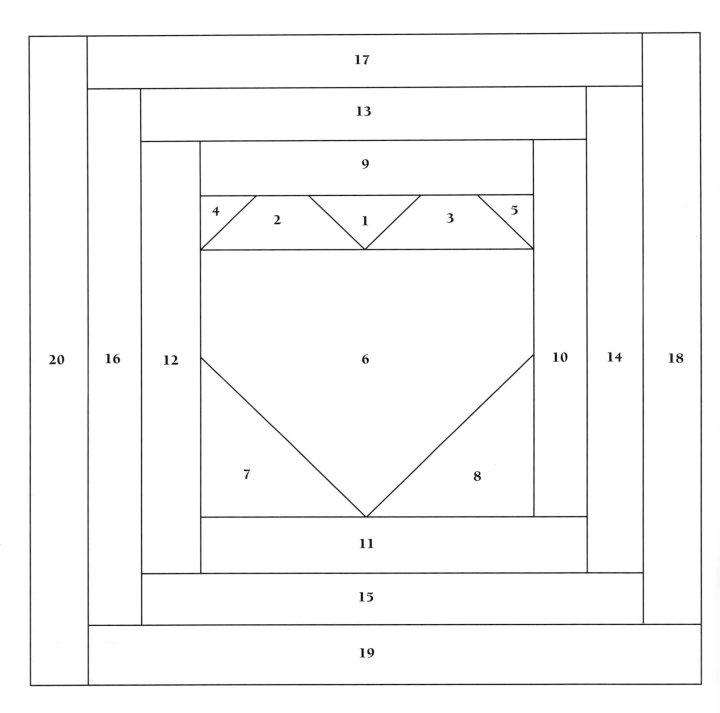

62 Large Courthouse Steps

							24							
							20							
							16							
							12							
							8							
							4							
22	18	14	10	6	2		1		3	7	11	15	19	23
							5							
							9							
							13							
							17							
							21							
							25							

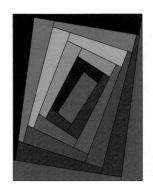

63 Tumbling Rectangle Log Cabin

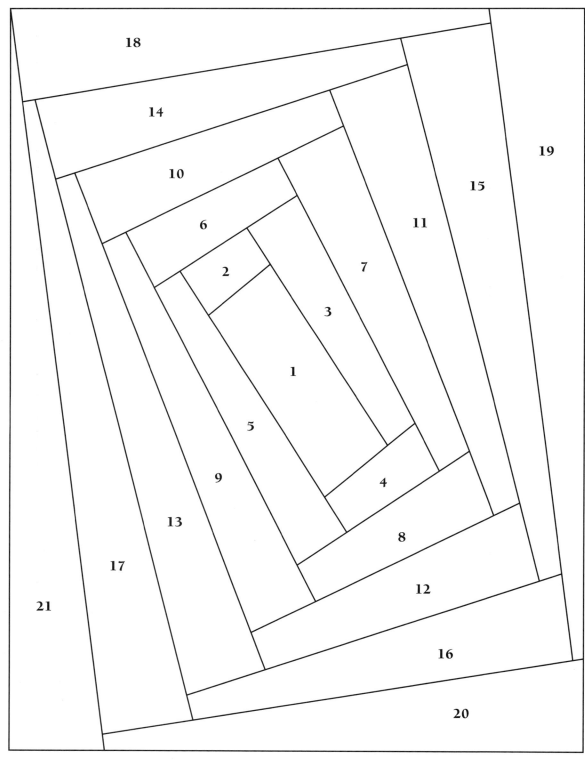

64 Log Cabin Corners

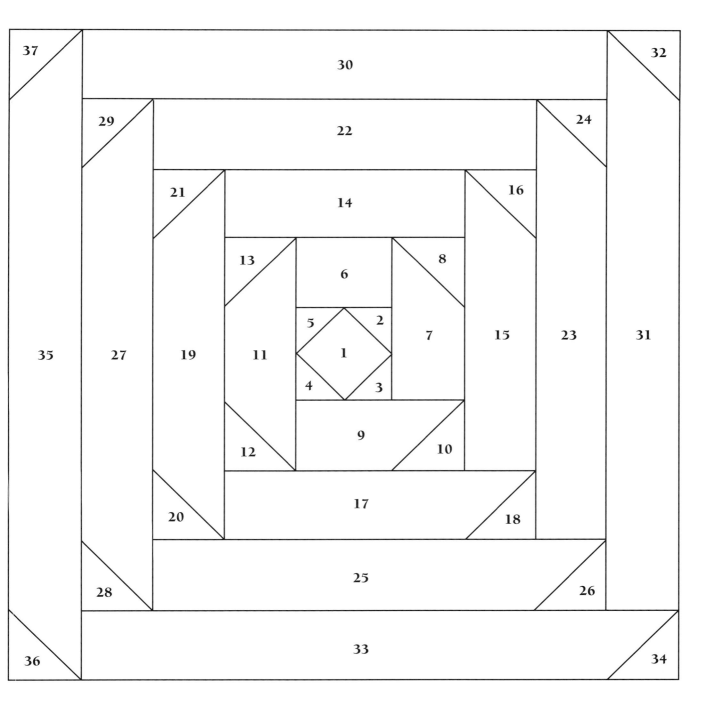

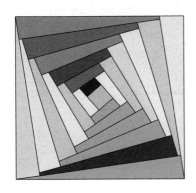

65 Toppling Log Cabin

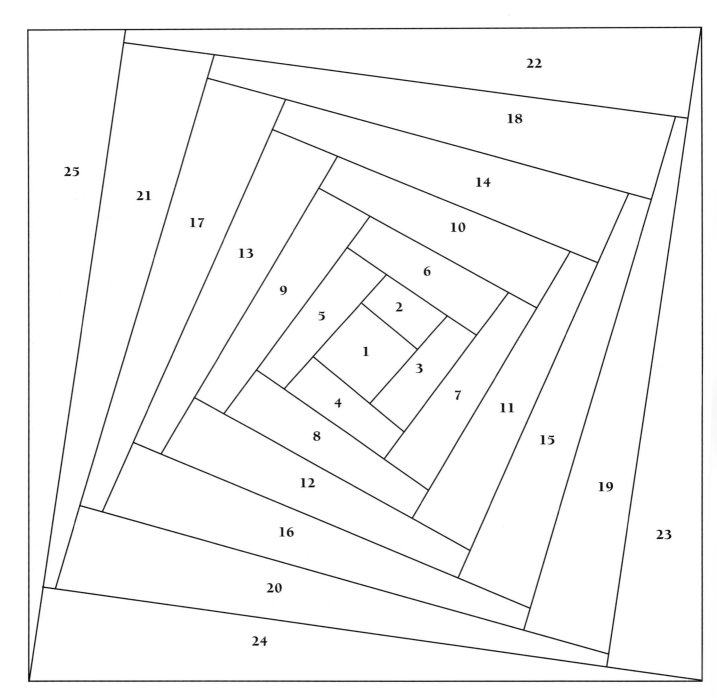

66 All Around the Cabin

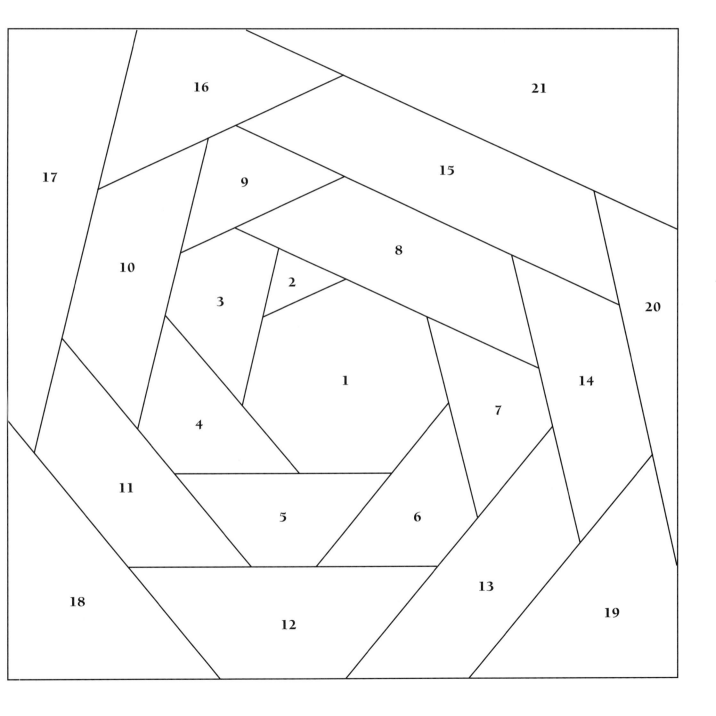

67 Crazy Cabin

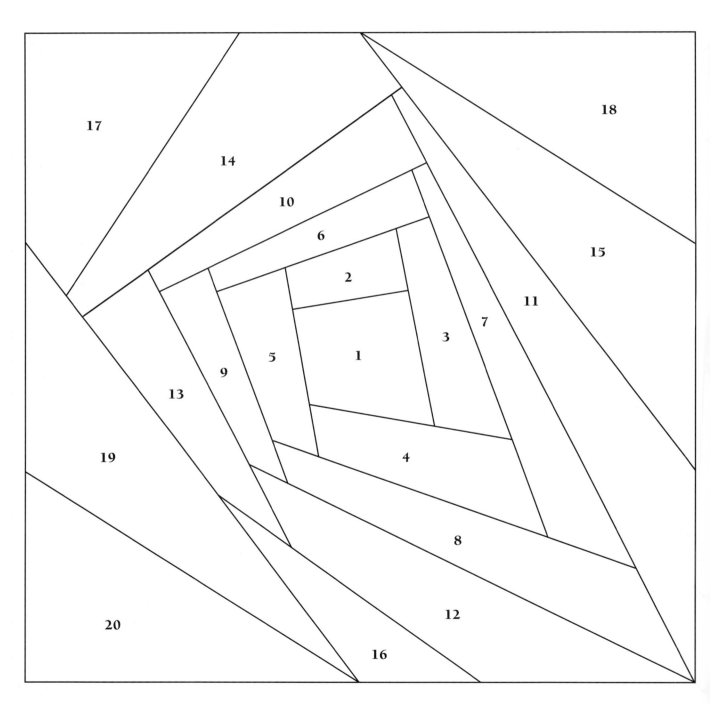

 # 68 Guardian Angel

Photographed block note: *Eyes were hand embroidered with three strands of blue-gray floss.*

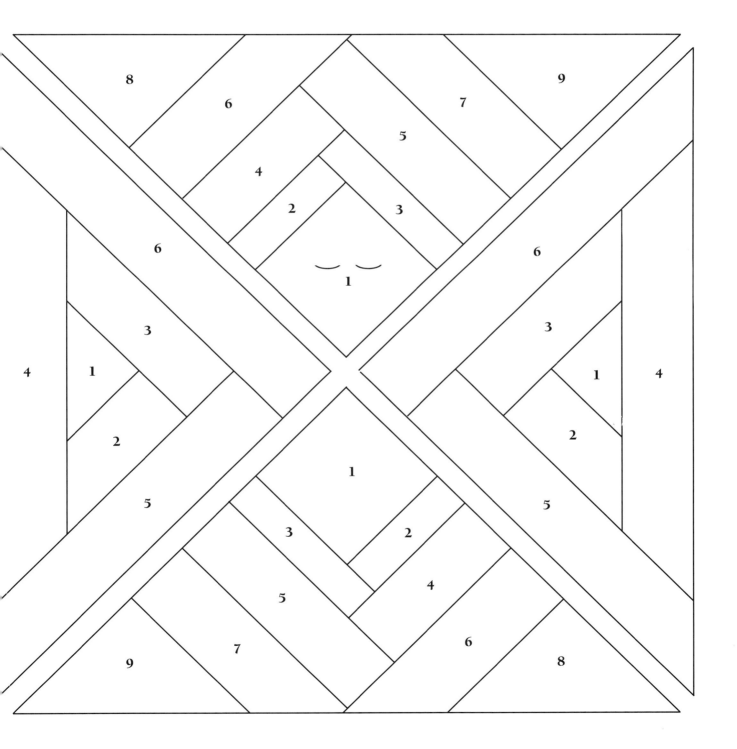

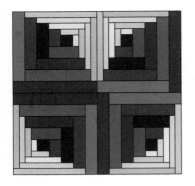

69 Curved Log Cabin Tulip

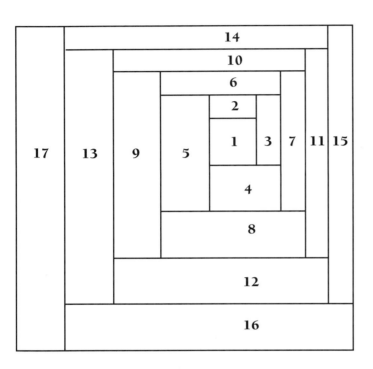

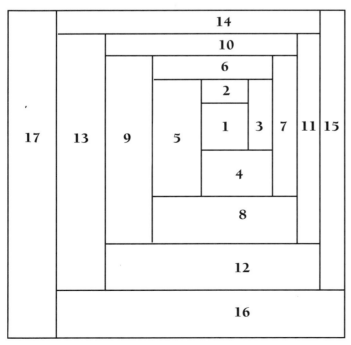

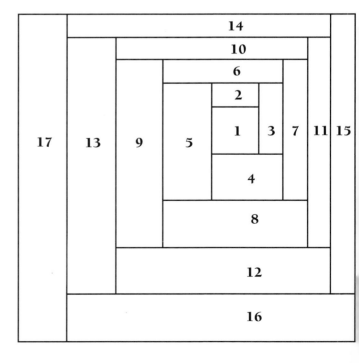

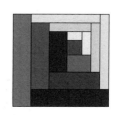
10	
6	
2	
3	1
7	5
11	9
4	13
8	
12	

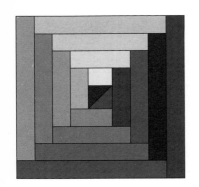

71 Half-Square Triangle in the Cabin

15

11

7

3

2

4   8   12   16

1

18   14   10   6

5

9

13

17

72 Cabin in the Meadow

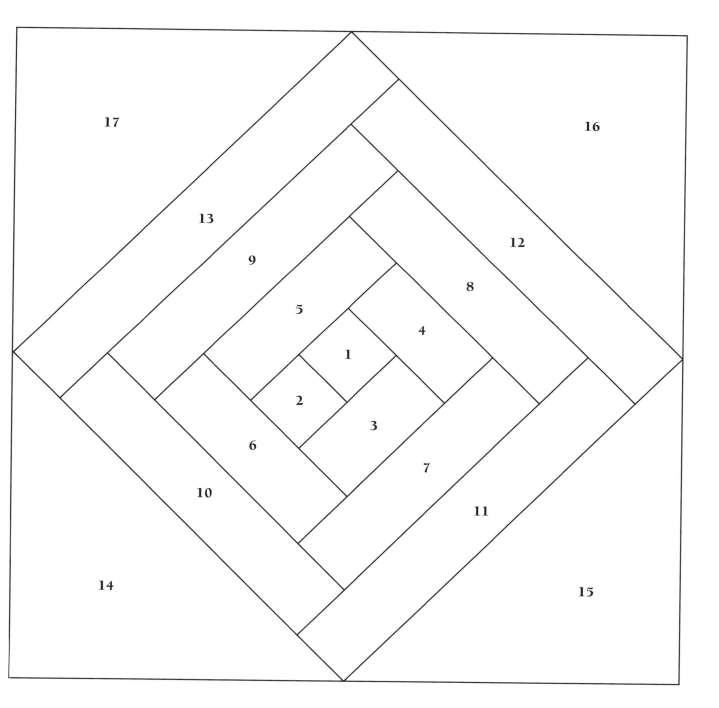

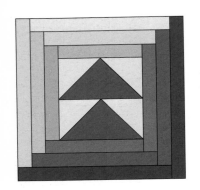

73 Geese in the Cabin

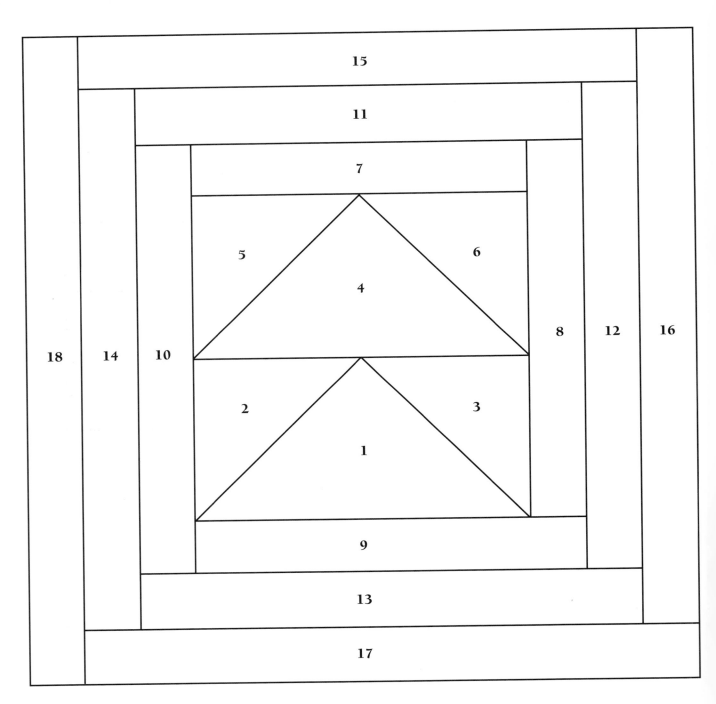

74 Rectangle in the Corner

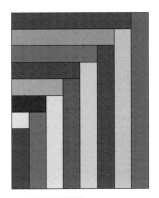

14

12

10

8

6

4

15

13

11

2

9

7

5

3

1

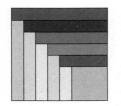

75 Petite Center in the Corner

 **Evening Star**

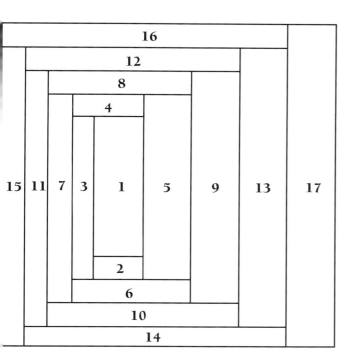

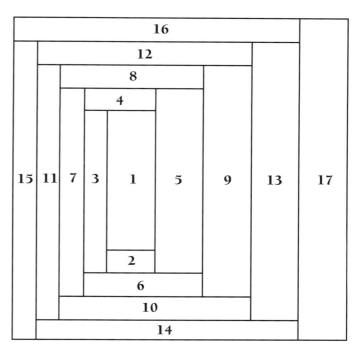

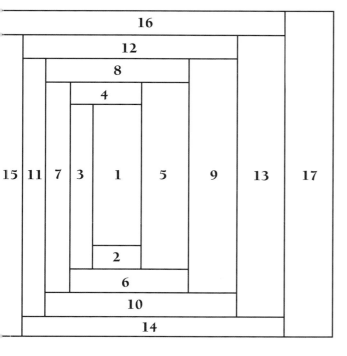

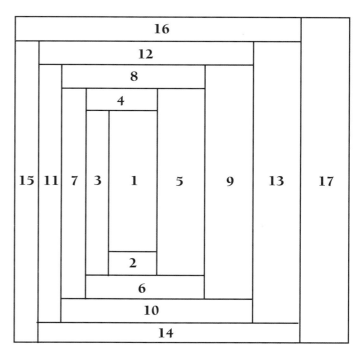

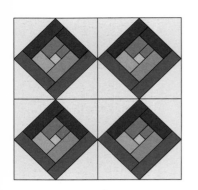

77 Log Cabin Community

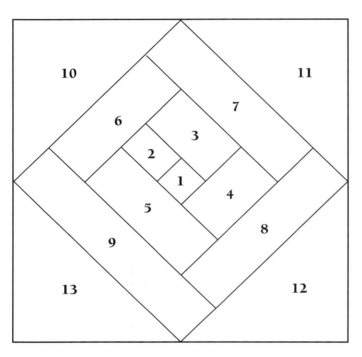

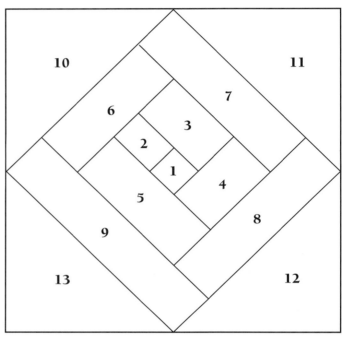

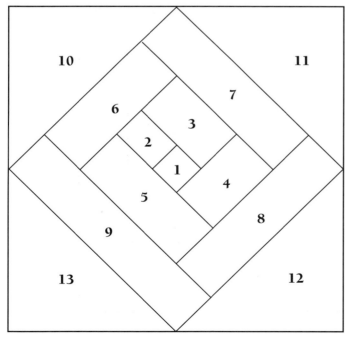

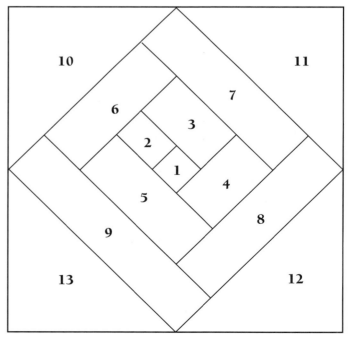

 Skyscraper Steps

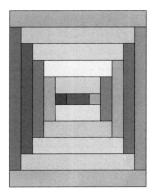

						20						
						16						
						12						
						8						
						4						
18	14	10	6	2		1	3		7	11	15	19
						5						
						9						
						13						
						17						
						21						

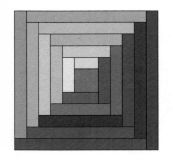

79 Medium Log Cabin

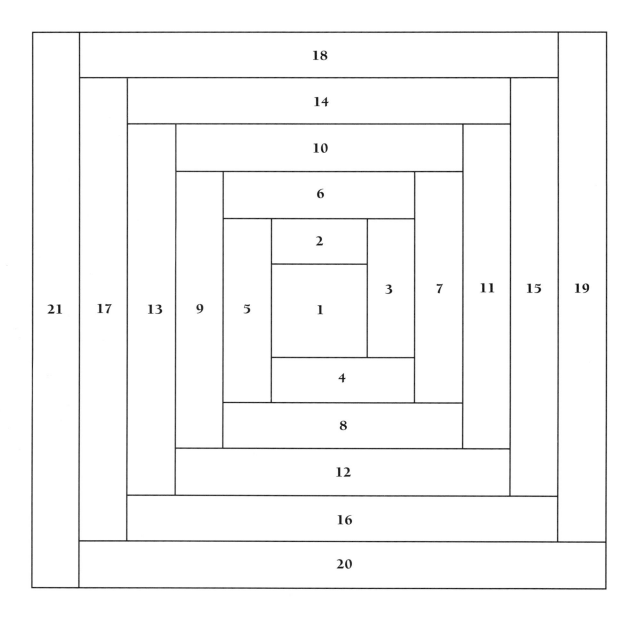

80 *Double Diamonds*

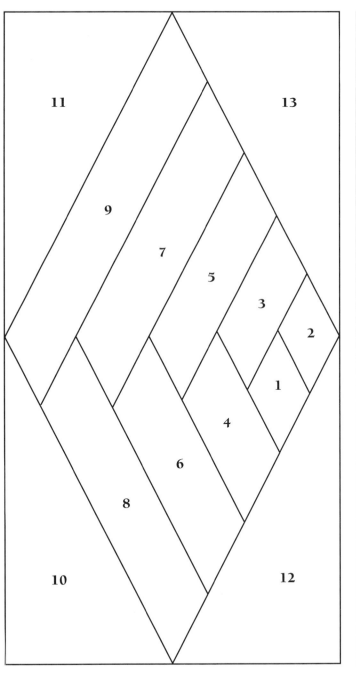

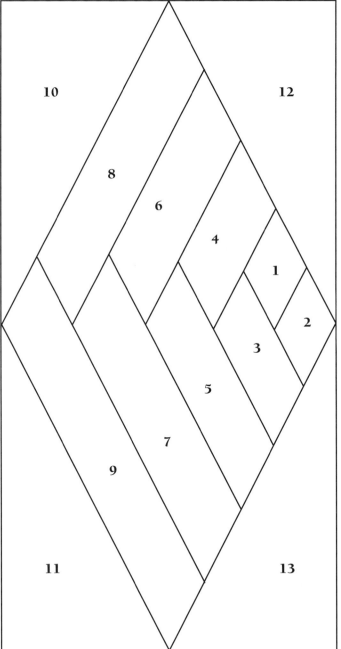

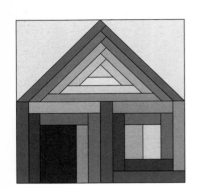

81 Log Cabin Cottage

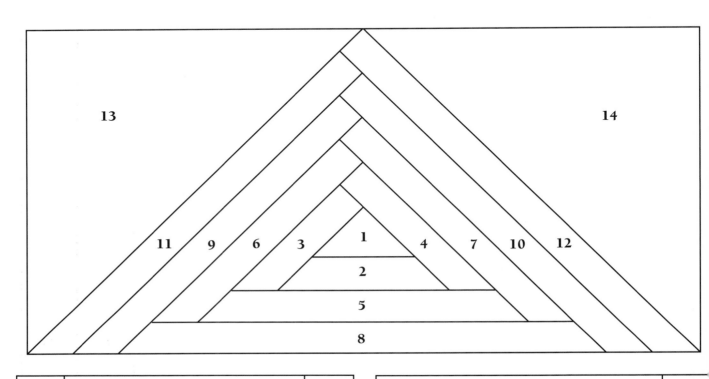

82 Square in a Square Log Cabin

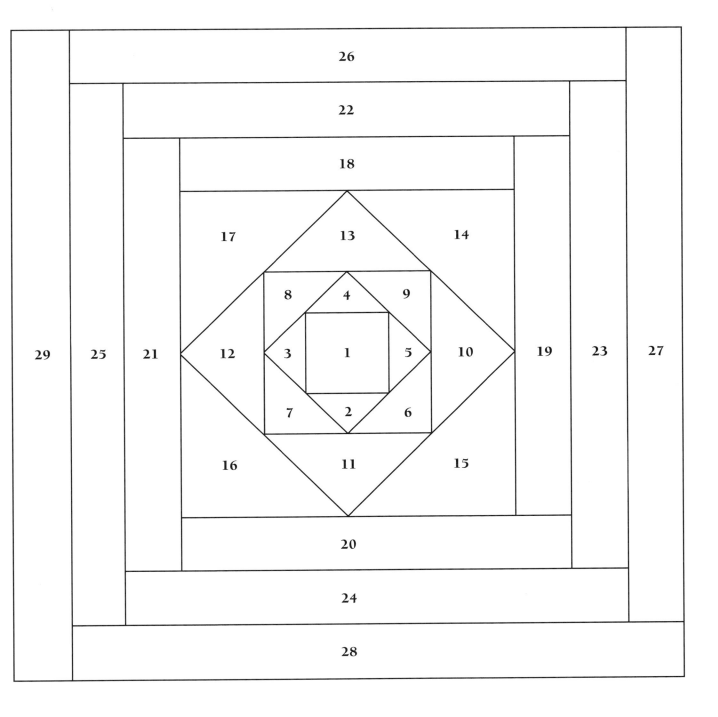

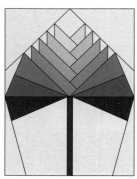

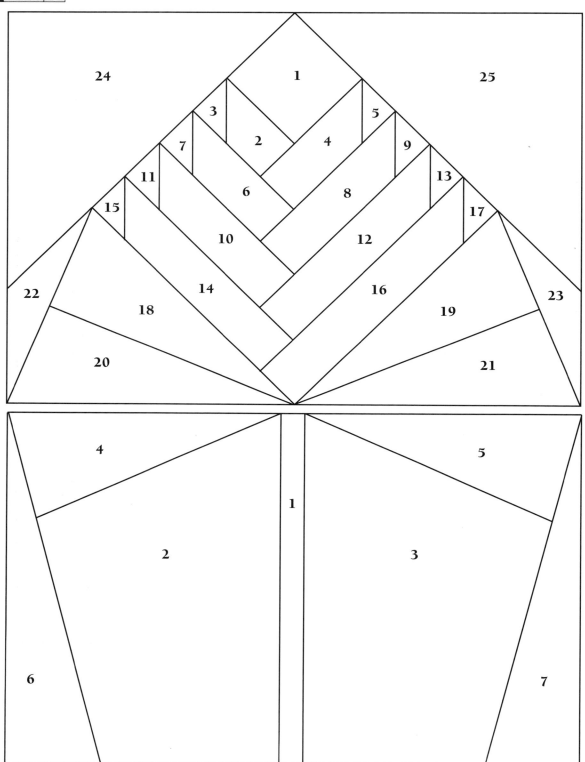

84 Log Cabin with a View

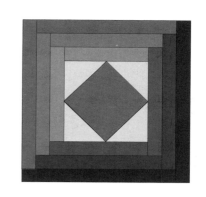

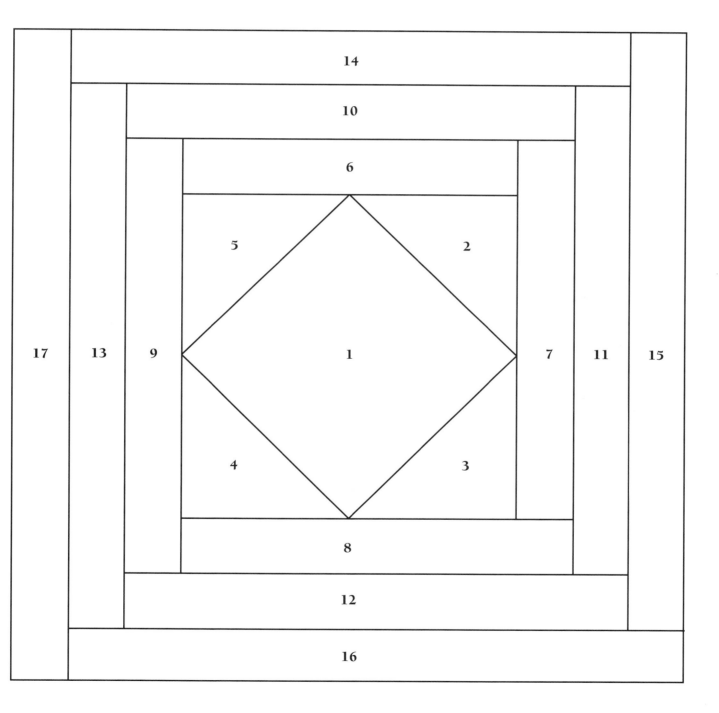

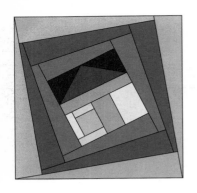

85 House in a Twister

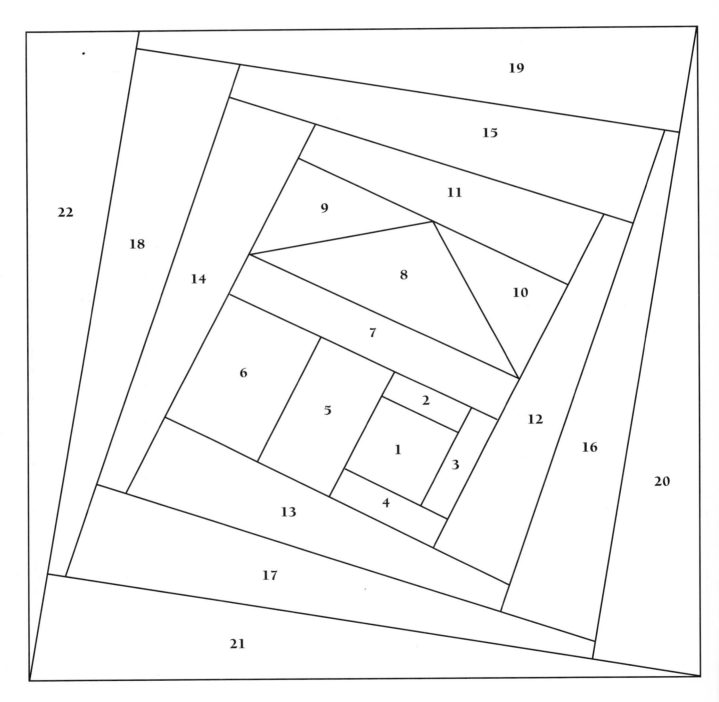

86 Cactus Flower

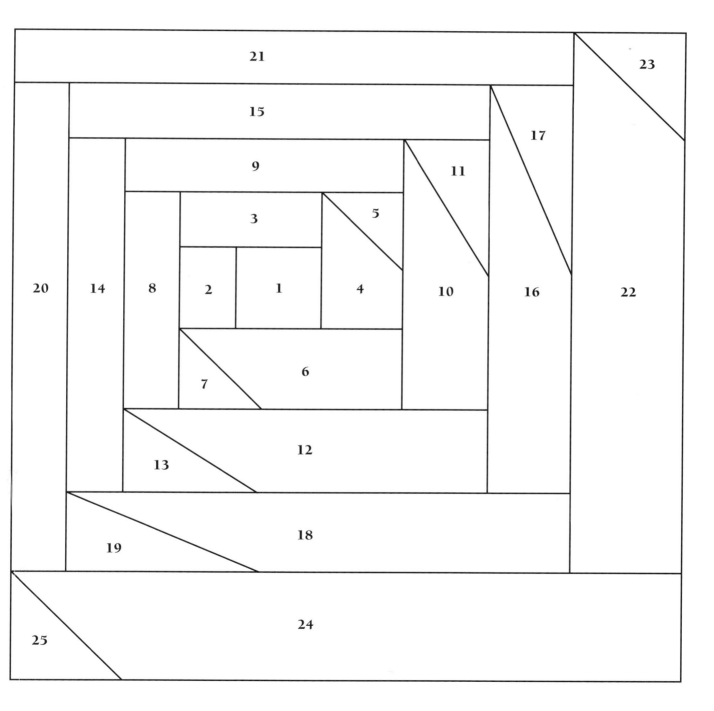

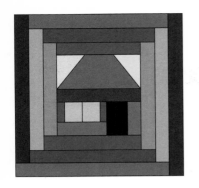

87 Cabin in the Cabin

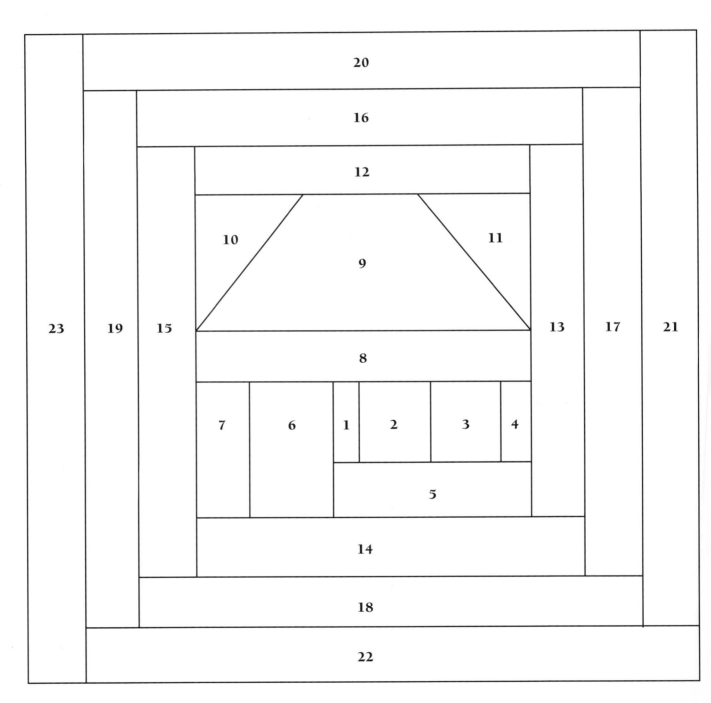

88 Petite Courthouse Steps

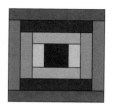

```
+---------------------------------------------------+
|                       12                          |
+---+-------------------------------------------+---+
|   |                   8                       |   |
|   +---+-----------------------------------+---+   |
|   |   |                 4                 |   |   |
|   |   +-------+-----------------+---------+   |   |
|   |   |       |                 |         |   |   |
|10 | 6 |   2   |        1        |    3    | 7 |11 |
|   |   |       |                 |         |   |   |
|   |   +-------+-----------------+---------+   |   |
|   |   |                 5                 |   |   |
|   +---+-----------------------------------+---+   |
|   |                   9                       |   |
+---+-------------------------------------------+---+
|                      13                           |
+---------------------------------------------------+
```

89 Off-Center Quartet

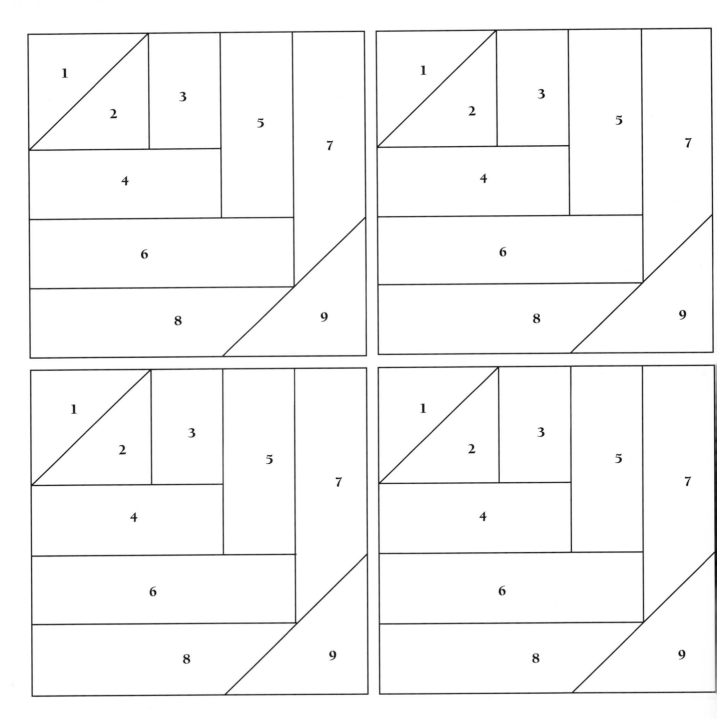

90 *Birdhouse in the Cabin*

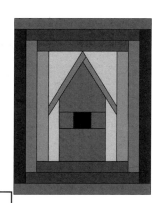

22

18

14

10 11

8 9

4

12 13 17 21

20 16

2 1 3

6 7

5

15

19

23

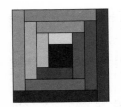

91 Petite Log Cabin

```
┌─────────────────────────────────────────────┐
│  │                                      │    │
│  │  ┌────────────────────────────────┐  │    │
│  │  │             10                 │  │    │
│  │  ├──────────────────────────┬─────┤  │    │
│  │  │            6             │     │  │    │
│  │  │  ┌────────────────┬──────┤     │  │    │
│  │  │  │       2        │      │     │  │    │
│  │  │  ├────────┬───────┤      │     │  │    │
│13 │ 9│  5     │   1   │   3  │  7  │ 11 │
│  │  │  │        │       │      │     │  │    │
│  │  │  ├────────┴───────┤      │     │  │    │
│  │  │  │       4        │      │     │  │    │
│  │  │  ├────────────────┴──────┤     │  │    │
│  │  │  │            8             │   │  │    │
│  │  ├──┴──────────────────────────┤   │  │    │
│  │  │            12                │  │    │
│  └──┴───────────────────────────────┘ │    │
└─────────────────────────────────────────────┘
```

106

92 Large Log Cabin

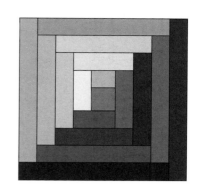

| 14 |
| 10 |
| 6 |
| 2 |
| 3 | 7 | 11 | 15 |
| 17 | 13 | 9 | 5 | 1 |
| 4 |
| 8 |
| 12 |
| 16 |

93 Petite Pineapple

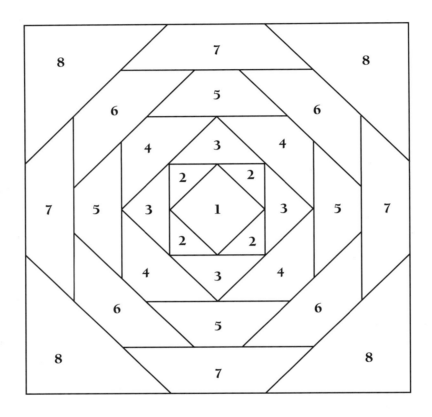

94 Hexagon Log Cabin

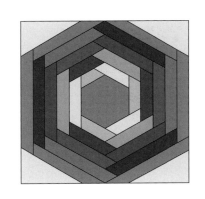

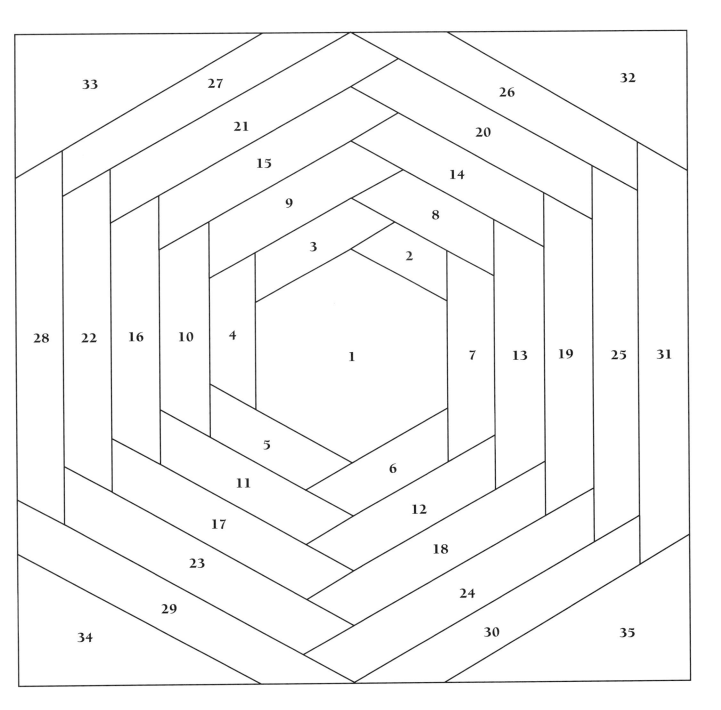

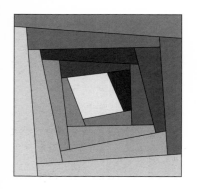

95 Spiral Staircase

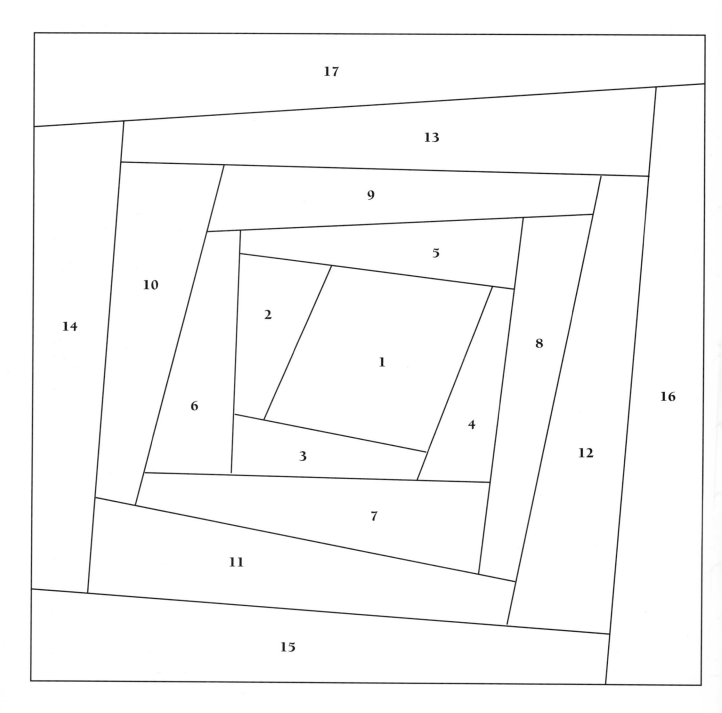

96 Pineapple on Point

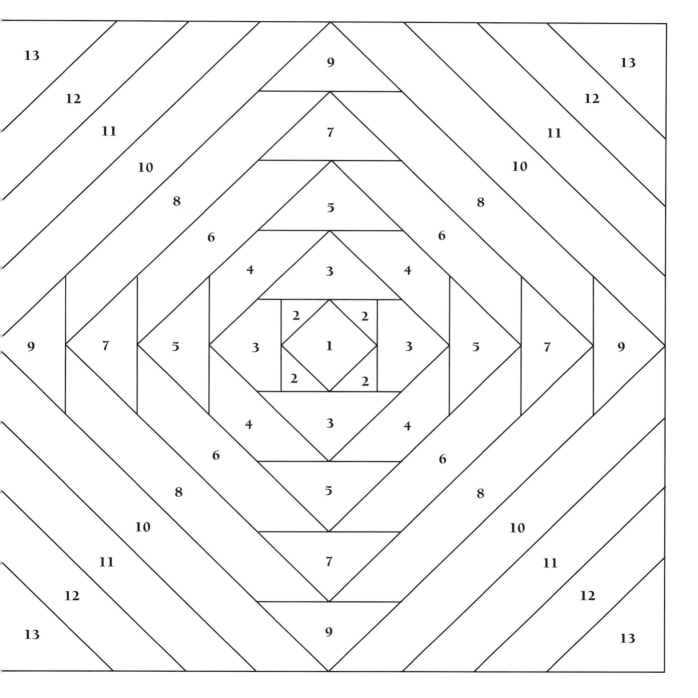

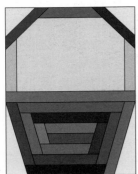

97 Flower Basket

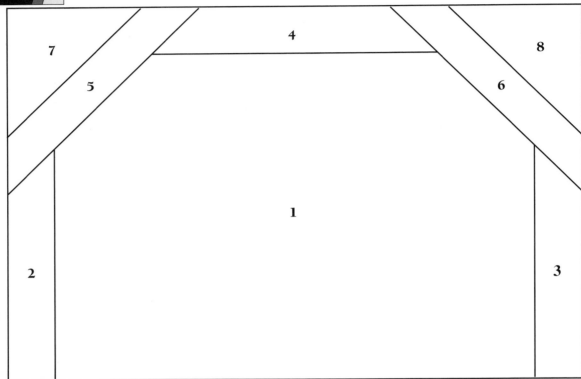

7

5

4

8

6

1

2

3

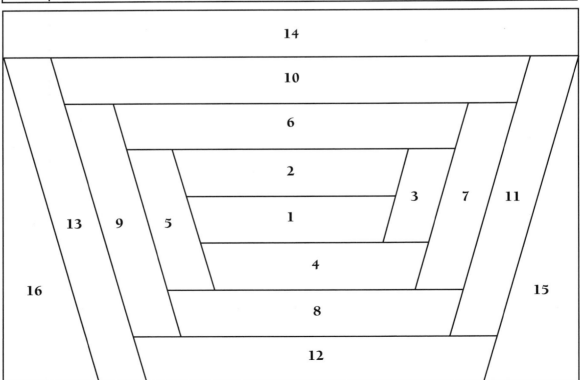

14

10

6

2

1

4

8

12

13

9

5

3

7

11

16

15

98 Log Cabin Playhouse

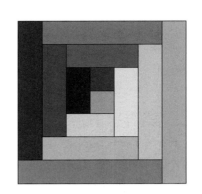

10

6

2

3

7

11

13

9

5

1

4

8

12

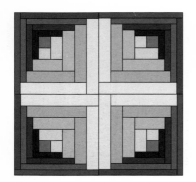

99 Curved Log Cabin Nosegay

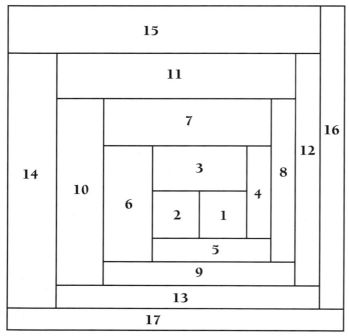

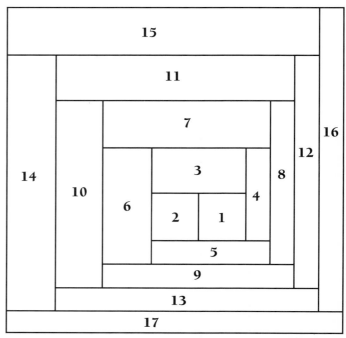

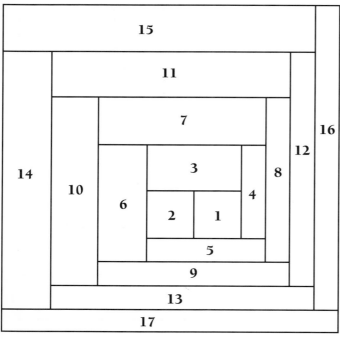

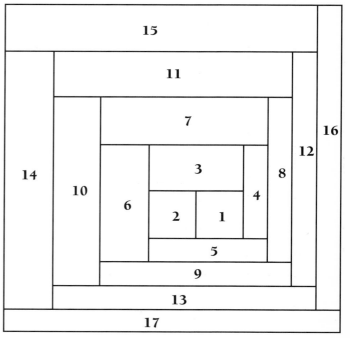

100 Home with Siding

| 22 |
| 18 |
| 14 |
| 10 |
| 6 |
| 2 |

| 25 | 21 | 17 | 13 | 9 | 5 | 1 | 3 | 7 | 11 | 15 | 19 | 23 |

| 4 |
| 8 |
| 12 |
| 16 |
| 20 |
| 24 |

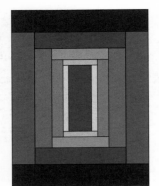

101 Two-Story Log Cabin

16
12
8
4

| 14 | 10 | 6 | 2 | 1 | 3 | 7 | 11 | 15 |

5
9
13
17